Twayne's English Authors Series

Sylvia E. Bowman, *Editor*

INDIANA UNIVERSITY

Rose Macaulay

(TEAS) **85**

ROSE MACAULAY

by

ALICE R. BENSEN

Rose Macaulay's witty and moving best-seller, *The Towers of Trebizond* (1956), climaxed her fifty years of writing novels, poems, travel books, essays, criticism, reviews, and assorted journalism. Professor Bensen's study is the first full-length book devoted to her work.

By birth a member of the English "intellectual aristocracy," Rose Macaulay was educated at Oxford and received an Honorary Doctorate of Letters from Cambridge. She was made a Dame Commander of the British Empire in 1958.

Her travel writings, chiefly on the Mediterranean world, impart her sense of the successive civilizations that have lived along those coasts and of the ironies of their history. In the 1930's she wrote a study of Milton and a distinguished historical novel on the mid-seventeenth century in England. Her book on her friend E. M. Forster was the first full-length study of that writer.

Rose Macaulay's writing is characterized by stylistic mastery, a lively inventiveness, perceptiveness, erudition, and saneness. Professor Bensen presents the works in chronological order, evaluates them, and, by quoting contemporary comment, affords a sense of the interplay of the author, her literary associates, and her public.

Rose Macaulay

By Alice R. Bensen

Eastern Michigan University

Twayne Publishers, Inc.   ::   New York

ABOUT THE AUTHOR

After receiving her Bachelor's an
Master's from Washington University, i
St. Louis, Alice R. Bensen attended th
Sorbonne, in Paris, for a year. In 194
she received her Doctorate from the Un
versity of Chicago. She taught for seve:
years at Valparaiso University, the
moved to Eastern Michigan University i
1947. Her publications include article
on the techniques of Rose Macaulay an
other twentieth-century fiction writer:
and on poetic diction, in such journal
as *PMLA, Modern Fiction Studies,* an
English Literature in Transition. Lik
Rose Macaulay, she is interested i
travel; she has made a dozen trips t
Europe and has traveled widely in Asia
Africa, and South America.

Contents

ROSE MACAULAY

Preface

From 1906 until 1958 Rose Macaulay was a lively presence in English letters; and, since her death, her books continue to be republished. Although often listed for convenience as a "novelist," she was a writer of more general scope. Living and enjoying, she was moved to comment on the world that she observed: to deride, admonish, and speculate; and to recreate and project–often fantastically–many aspects of it in twenty-three works of fiction; in an astonishing number of essays, articles, studies, and reviews; in poems; and in travel books.

As this book is the first published full-length study of her writing, my aim is–to use a Boswellism–to "exhibit" her works: to present them in some detail, to relate them to their background, to point out their characteristics, and to indicate their quality. Because of Rose Macaulay's active role in literary London as a creator, commentator, and reviewer, I have included–in relation to each book–excerpts from contemporary comments, from the reviews of her first novel in 1906 to those of her books in the 1950's; I should like to give a sense of the interplay of her, her literary associates, and her public.

Since her fiction and essays form a related commentary on the lines of thought of the passing decades, they are best presented in chronological order. The character of her work is remarkably uniform, but different emphases appear at different times. The quality varies somewhat, of course, from piece to piece, and from passage to passage within a single piece; but there is no five-year period without its work of distinction. Because of limitations of space, I have passed with only brief mention two novels and one book of literary study; and I have given only slight attention to two other novels and a non-fiction work.

In this study, the various aspects of her thought and writing are discussed in connection with specific works. Some general comments are made at the beginning of each of the chronological sections. As her writing had many close connections with her life, a somewhat detailed biographical sketch is included.

I am indebted to a number of people for their help. To Rose Macaulay's cousin, Miss Constance Babington Smith, for her generosity with her biographical material and for her suggestions; to Miss Jean Macaulay for her interest. To several of Rose Macaulay's friends who have been very helpful, and particularly Father Gerard Irvine, Dr. C. V. Wedgwood, and Mr. Raymond Mortimer; to Miss Lorna Moore, of the B.B.C., who arranged for me to hear recordings of Rose Macaulay's broadcasts; to Miss Margaret Stephens; and to Mrs. Jerrard Tickell. To the administration of the British Museum for the use of their facilities; and to White Hall Hotel in Montague Street for permitting me to typewrite. To the administration of Eastern Michigan University for granting me two semester leaves; and to Professor Hoover Jordan, my department chairman, for his encouragement and scheduling arrangements. And, finally, to Mr. Philip Rizzo, without the existence of whose bibliography much more time would have been required.

ALICE R. BENSEN

Eastern Michigan University

Chronology

1881   Emilie Rose Macaulay born August 1 at Rugby.

1887   Removal of family to Varazze, Italy.

1894   Return of family to England–to Oxford. Attended the High School until 1899.

1900- Attended Somerville College, Oxford.
1903

1903   To Aberystwyth, where father was a lecturer at the university.

1905   Some poems published in the *Westminster Gazette*.

1906   To Great Shelford, near Cambridge, where father was a lecturer at the university. First novel published: *Abbots Verney*.

1909   Brother Aulay murdered on North-West Frontier.

1912   First Hellenic cruise. Sixth novel, *The Lee Shore*, awarded prize of one thousand pounds.

1913   Her "Annus Mirabilis": now spending much of her time in London.

1914   War work near Cambridge: nurse in Voluntary Aid Detachment; land-girl. First book of poetry published: *Two Blind Countries*.

1915   Father died; mother left Cambridge for Beaconsfield. Definitive move to London; took job in War Office.

1917   About this time made the acquaintance that later developed into life-long attachment.

1921   Eleventh novel, *Dangerous Ages*, awarded Femina-Vie Heureuse prize. Frequent trips to the Continent during the next decades.

1929   December, 1929-January, 1930: trip to America.

1941   May: her flat and most of her belongings destroyed in bombing raid.

1942   Death of lover. During 1942-1945, frequent illnesses and periods in hospital.

1947   July–August: took the trip recorded in *Fabled Shore*.

1950 Beginning of the correspondence with Father Johnson.
1951 June: Honorary Doctorate of Letters from Cambridge University.
1953 May-June: trip to Cyprus and Middle East.
1954 June: trip to Turkey resulting in *The Towers of Trebizond*.
1956 Twenty-third–and last–novel published a month after her seventy-fifth birthday. Awarded James Black Tait prize.
1958 February: created a Dame Commander of the British Empire. August: cruise to Aegean Islands and Black Sea. Died, of a coronary thrombosis, October 30.

CHAPTER 1

Life

I Family

E MILIE ROSE MACAULAY was born at Rugby on August 1, 1881, the second of the seven children of George Macaulay, then an assistant master at the school, and of Grace Conybeare, his second cousin once removed. When Noel Annan wrote his study "The Intellectual Aristocracy," he chose Rose Macaulay as the living person with whom to start tracing the descent of the families of this class; the Macaulays and Conybeares, and the Roses, from whom the author had derived her middle name, were all part of this interrelated complex. The Conybeares "were for generations parsons and scholars descending from an Elizabethan schoolmaster."[1] Later members of the family included two geologists, a paleontologist, an Armenian scholar, and a master at Eton for nearly fifty years.

Rose Macaulay's grandfather, W. J. Conybeare, the noted contributor to the *Edinburgh Review*, had "married a daughter of Lydia Babington who was taught by her father to read each morning a chapter of the Old Testament in Hebrew and a chapter of the New Testament in Greek." Rose Macaulay was related to the Babingtons through her father's line also; the historian Thomas Babington Macaulay was a first cousin of her paternal grandfather. This grandfather and his father were both Anglican parsons; and, before them, there had been two generations of Scottish Presbyterian ministers. Among other families connected with Rose Macaulay's were the Trevelyans, Arnolds, and Huxleys.

Terminating the long line of Macaulay clergymen, Rose Macaulay's father and his two brothers, after graduating from Cambridge with high honors, chose other careers. "Uncle Willie" stayed at the university, becoming Vice-Provost of King's College where he was renowned, it is interesting to note, "for the astringent precision of his remarks."[2] "Uncle Regi" became a business director of considerable wealth. George Macaulay, a Christian agnostic, had given up his fellowship at Trinity in order to marry; after nine years as a master at Rugby, he took his wife and six children to live in Italy for the sake of her health.

II *Italy*

This period is described by Constance Babington Smith, a cousin and the editor of Rose Macaulay's letters:

For the next seven years the children ran blissfully wild; sea and shore were their home as much as the unconventional "Villa Macolai," where life was simple partly because the Macaulays were not well off. The children's education consisted mostly of lessons with their parents, though for a short time Margaret, Rose, and Jean attended the local convent school. The years in Italy, when "Rosy" grew from a child of six into a gauche tomboy of thirteen, set the course for much of her later development. The love of the sea-shore and of bathing, the attachment to "abroad," especially the Mediterranean countries, the happy-go-lucky untidy ways, the frugal standards of living, the boyish hobbies, the farouche demeanour–all these can be traced to Varazze. (*L*, 13)

In the letters to Father Johnson, written in her seventies, Rose Macaulay often referred to this period: "The birthday I shall never forget was a rapturous day in Italy, when we were first given a canoe, and navigated it in the calm summer sea from morning till evening . . ." (*L*, 324); the canoe was named the *Argo*.[3] She recalls the procession on Corpus Christi and the picnic on Candlemas with "sunshine and almond blossom and tiny twisted candles to burn, and the procession in the town, and brothers and sisters to feast on the hillside with. Those *festa* days–of which Sunday was the most often recurrent, always a holiday, always fun, always in one's oldest clothes so that one could get wet and climb about . . ." (*LL*, 76). At Varazze the three older girls and their two younger brothers constituted a tight clan–"the five."

III *Adolescence, Education*

A painful adolescence followed. The family moved back to

England, to Oxford, where the daughters attended the High School and the father worked on his four-volume edition of the Latin, French, and English works of John Gower. Rose was loth to become a conventional Victorian girl; and, though she was "the prettiest of the three [older sisters] as well as the gayest," she was "desperately shy" with strangers (*LL*, 15). In a private interview with the vicar before her confirmation, she recalled, "what I *wanted* to ask was, 'as I really can't believe all this as I should, ought I to be confirmed?' but . . . I could say nothing at all" (*L*, 120).

Then, when she was nineteen, "Uncle Regi," her godfather, made it possible for her to attend the university. And, as Constance Babington Smith writes, "During her three years at Somerville College, Oxford, . . . a remarkable change came about in her. The painfully shy and awkward young girl became a vivacious talker and letter-writer, an adventurer in ideas and experiences, a popular companion who made friends wherever she went" (*LL*, 14-15). She was tall and "slender to thinness," as she remained for the rest of her life, and had "very pale blue eyes and a delicate fair complexion."[4] As a student she read history: "At Oxford I took the whole of English history (one has to) . . . but my Special Period, and my Foreign Period, was the 17th century. We had to do Political Science and Polit. Economy, too. I was much interested in most of it; unfortunately I fell ill at the wrong moment and got an Aegrotat [the unclassified degree granted to a candidate who is prevented by illness from attending examinations], which was disappointing. I liked Oxford; the river, work, people, Oxford itself, even hockey, at which I was good" (*L*, 94-95).

IV *Life and Writing*

From 1903, when she came down from Oxford, she lived with her family for three years near Aberystwyth, Wales, where her father had an appointment. To entertain herself in what seemed an exile, she wrote a novel; *Abbots Verney* was published in 1906 and received numerous and good reviews. In the same year her father was appointed to a lectureship at his own university, Cambridge; and the family found itself once again in a stimulating environment. Rose continued to write and publish. Then in 1909 word came that her brother Aulay had been murdered by thieves on the North-West Frontier of India. Jean had already become a nurse; at this tragic news Rose "impulsively . . . offered herself as a missionary to the Universities' Mission to Central Africa, but her offer was declined, on grounds that she was unsuited for the work" (L, 16). Her oldest sister shortly after became an Anglican Deaconess, and in 1912 her youngest sister went to India as a teacher (later a missionary). While the evangelical tradition of this class moved her sisters in these directions, Rose began to share more deeply in her mother's "Catholic" ritualistic interpretation of Anglicanism, which she had been taught as a child and which the feast-days at Varazze had adorned with beauty and mystery. She also spent more time with her scholarly father and accompanied him on several trips to the Continent.

In 1912 her sixth novel, *The Lee Shore*, was awarded a thousand pound literary prize. In these years she had been visiting London more frequently; and Naomi Royde Smith, the literary editor of the *Westminster Gazette*, was bringing her into a circle of poets, novelists, and journalists that included Walter de la Mare, E. V. Knox, J. C. Squire, John Middleton Murry, Hugh Walpole, and many others. Appreciatively, her "Uncle Regi" gave her a tiny flat off Chancery Lane. In 1914 she published *The Making of a Bigot*, her seventh novel, a presentation of this London life, and also *The Two Blind Countries*, a book of some of the poems that she had composed through the years.

The war appeared to Rose an unspeakable return to primitivism. She worked briefly as a V.A.D.–an amateur nurse with the Voluntary Aid Detachment–and as a land-girl; but these jobs suited her neither mentally nor physically. At her father's death in 1915, she moved definitively to London and took a post in the War Office. During this period, she "fell in love with a man who, she later learnt, was already married. . . . For nearly twenty years, until his death during the second world war, he was the dominant influence in her life. They met frequently in London and also abroad and her attachment became well known to her sisters and to her mother (who died in 1925) but was seldom discussed. Among her intimate friends in London the companionship was tacitly accepted, but outside Rose's immediate circle nothing was known of it" (*L,* 18-19).[5]

So her life continued with the writing of frequent novels and an astonishing number of articles and reviews; with travel–to the Continent, and once to America, and with friendships and parties in an "ever widening circle of intellectual friends." She became famous for her "wit and sparkling satire as well as for her wide erudition."

Early in the period of World War II her older sister died, and soon after that in May, 1941, her flat was bombed; all her library and some unpublished manuscripts–almost all of her possessions– were destroyed. The following year, the man she loved became fatally ill and died. After these shattering experiences, she herself became seriously ill. She did not attempt fiction during the war, but worked at research on some pieces of non-fiction, including two history-travel books. The second travel book, *Fabled Shore,* involved a courageous trip alone, in an old car, along the coast of Spain in 1947, before tourists had found that region–a time when such an adventure still could and did arouse medieval, Moorish reaction. In 1950, just before her sixty-ninth birthday, she published *The World My Wilderness,* a novel expressing the desolation and loneliness of this decade.

V *Last Years*

Returning from a Mediterranean trip that summer, she found a letter from an Anglican priest, Father Johnson, resident in Boston, Massachusetts, whom she had known slightly as a spiritual advisor before his departure in 1916 for America. The letter was an appreciation of *They Were Defeated* (1932), her historical novel on poetry, philosophy, and the Church in the England of the mid-seventeenth century. Responding, Rose explained her case of conscience to him; and, under his guidance, she made a formal confession and returned, after an absence of three decades, to the sacraments of the Church. (They discovered later on that they were cousins.) During the first two years of their correspondence she wrote enough letters to make up a volume, and she continued to write, with gaps due to illness, overwork, and travel, until her death in 1958. They compared their preferred form of worship–high Anglican–with many other forms and engaged in detailed discussion of translations of religious writings from Greek and Latin. From this experience and from her Near Eastern travel arose her final and most widely read work of fiction, thought by many to be her best, *The Towers of Trebizond,* completed just before her seventy-fifth birthday.

Rose's letters to Father Johnson contain vivid recollections of her early life and lively descriptions of her current activities ("... she is never *not* a humorist," he declared [L, 22]), which included constant writing, frequent participation in radio programs, swimming almost daily, going to mass daily, going to parties and seeing countless friends of all ages, receiving a Doctorate of Letters from Cambridge in 1951, and being "Damed" in February, 1958. Later that spring she broke a wrist and hip through a misstep while chatting with friends in front of a church, but she was able to take another trip to Turkey in the late summer. In the last days of October she had a recurrence of bronchitis, did not stay in bed, and died on October 30 of a coronary thrombosis, at the age of seventy-seven.

CHAPTER 2

Fiction, 1906-1916

I Abbots Verney

ROSE MACAULAY saw her first novel, *Abbots Verney*, published in 1906, when she was twenty-five. Not surprisingly, it is a *Bildungsroman*–a study of a young person's maturation: "its design," as the writer of a lengthy review in the *Scotsman* (December 7, 1906, 3) remarked, "is to display the gradual development of a character with strong, original potentialities, placed in a singular and trying situation, under the play of circumstance, from early boyhood to the close of the plastic period of youth." *Abbots Verney* is the only one of her novels to follow the tradition of using a place-name or person's name for its title; in this instance, the title is a pun: Abbots Verney is the name of an ancestral home, young Verney Ruth is the presumptive heir and the ostensible frame of the plot is the question of whether he indeed "belongs" to the family tradition–whether he will indeed inherit.

And, like the title, the working out of the plot is not that of simple tradition: the heir makes good but is denied his inheritance; the young man comes to merit the love of the young woman he has chosen, but he does not win it. The novel is bursting with the author's unorthodox ideas–those of a clever young woman recently down from Oxford. And her treatment of her main theme, the harm done by narrow-mindedness and obstinacy–both of them aspects of "stupidity," which one character declares is "at the root of most of the troubles of the world" (308)–is a mixture of the tragic and the mocking.

Old Colonel Ruth, Verney's grandfather, is true to the type of his forebears: "Their type has been clear cut–a type of which gallant gentlemen and brave soldiers are made, who take honor and courage for their gods, and walk very straight and boldly through life, without looking much to the right side or to the left. This singleness of eye is often found in certain strong and simple natures, who will deal in no subtleties either of the conscience or of the brain. . . . Undeviating singleness of purpose and an uncompromisingly strong moral sense, when not tempered by any striking breadth or complexity of intellect, are apt to crystallize as obstinacy" (2).

The old soldier, therefore, is unable to dissociate his young grandson from the image of Verney's father, the Colonel's older son, Meyrick Ruth.[1] Unlike the younger son, Donald, a naval captain, Meyrick had repeatedly disgraced himself–in school, at Oxford, and in the army–by embezzlement, forgery, and cardsharping. Donald's sons are upright and slow; young Verney, as a series of lively episodes indicates, is upright and intelligent; but to his grandfather his cleverness is a taint, and only the persistent intervention of broader minds persuades the Colonel to permit the gifted boy to share with his cousins the moral perils of Eton and Oxford.

Meyrick, unquestionably a cad, has charm, quickness, and sophistication. When, during one of his brief periods of luck, he comes to Oxford and makes himself known to his son, Verney welcomes his father as good company and becomes fond of him. This imprudent decency arouses the old Colonel's wrath, but Verney insists that "people have a right to be taken at what they show of themselves. . . . 'Tisn't one's business to judge the people one knows; you can just take what you like and leave what you don't, fortunately" (61-62). The Colonel cannot see that Verney by no means condones his father's trespasses, and Verney is too obstinate to defend himself against the Colonel's thick-headed imputations of moral laxity. The young man's pride is too much hurt, and the old man lacks imagination.

The story shifts to Rome–the Italy of Henry James rather than of the Macaulay children–where Verney has a fellowship to study archaeology, a field of activity foreign to the Ruths. Here various episodes are concerned with the question, related to the Verney-Meyrick plot (and perhaps derived from Jane Austen's *Emma*?) of whether it is decent for one to offer advice to others; and, if one does, what psychological results are likely to ensue. The discussions of the incidents take place between various young people; the novelist has not yet learned to avoid undue repetition; and, furthermore, some of the discussions are too much like the "hashing over" of events by girls late at night in a dormitory–realistic enough, but somewhat out of key with the wider aim of the rest of the novel.

One of these young women, however–Rosamund Ilbert–is a remarkable creation, an idealized type that recurs in Rose Macaulay's writing, with slight modifications, from this heroine of 1906 to an appreciation of a Valencian statue of an "ironic" Madonna in *Fabled Shore* of 1949. Rosamund is in complete command of herself; she is elegant, imperious, with an "elusive spirit of whimsical mockery"; sometimes there is "weariness in her voice, the touch of bitterness". She declares: "Most of life is a sort of *pis-aller*,"–a making the best of a poor thing–but she views it with "perpetually amused eyes" (88-99, 293-94). "Amused" describes the intellectual response of a keen mind in a world that, taken *au grand sérieux,* can but disappoint; and the term came to be one of Rose Macaulay's chief motifs. Although elegant, Rosamund is unconcerned with convention; she goes out alone before dawn (perhaps vindicating Henry James's Daisy Miller–see Ch. II, n. 2) to a place overlooking the Forum to await the sight of the Roman sunrise. With her independence of judgment, she is one of the few who refuse to suspect Verney of collusion when Meyrick is publicly accused of habitually cheating at cards. For Verney, despite his grandfather's threats of disinheritance, has reasserted his right to accept his prodigal father as a social companion–has, in fact, been keeping his father–suspecting nothing of Meyrick's return to dishonest practices.

The study of the relations between the old Colonel, Verney, and Meyrick is remarkable psychologically and ethically. Verney, completely upright, feels affection for his father and enjoys his social gaiety; Meyrick is, in fact, widely accepted by those who know his shady character, for he is a most entertaining dinner and gambling companion. But Verney, despite his tolerance, will not concur in his father's cynical attitude toward the worldly wisdom of placating the grandfather; nor will he join in his grandfather's bitter discussions of his father. Verney's ethical code in personal relations is the one Rose Macaulay would set forth; but she makes clear that imagination, leading to mercy, is also needed. The grandfather, although loving his grandson and taking pride in his achievements, almost masochistically allows his moral fears to throttle his natural feelings. Verney, in turn, has been too often morally insulted by his grandfather to admit to the old gentleman that he had erred and done some harm in receiving Meyrick; besides, his apology will be interpreted as a plea for money. It is Rosamund who makes the obstinate young man see that "the old" find "everything infinitely more difficult than the young" (292); and her discussion persuades him to accept the hazard of more insults to his pride and to return home. Many pages of psychological acuteness probe the conflicts of love and wounded pride in the grandfather and the grandson. Their final conversation takes place when the old man is on his deathbed:

> "I'm awfully sorry," Verney said abruptly. Such an apology his grandfather had waited for for nine months. But he amplified it–quali-fied it, rather; even now he must have the thing clear between them. "I mean," he said, "I'm sorry I was such an ass about it, specially afterwards. But I couldn't promise even now not to be with him"–he fought oddly shy of the mention of his father–"if he wanted me to be. After all, one must, you see." He felt the position must be defined, even now, the arguing instinct rising.
> The Colonel's eyes were on his face sadly.
> "I know," he said, with a surprising sober gentleness . . . . But he does not know; "the wall still stood. . . . And the elder saw the younger with a curious distortion, as he was not" (362-63).

During his year in Rome, Verney, who had scorned emotional involvement with girls, one day "realized abruptly the wayward charm" of Rosamund's personality–"generous, carelessly gracious, wholly lovable" (189). Shame for his father's actions had kept him from courting her, and his attempt to repay his father's debts had reduced him to staying in such a miserable slum that he had caught the fever and nearly died. This physical equivalent of the dark night of the soul–an episode found in many nineteenth-century novels–was followed, as usual, by a convalescence paral-leled by spiritual growth. Verney's guide was Rosamund, who with firmness and wit, as well as with astonishing psychological subtlety, helped him to clarify his relations with his grandfather. But, when he turned the discussion to a declaration of his love for her, she made clear that she would not go beyond friendship with anyone. Neither she nor the author gives any reason for her attitude; it must be attributed either to the author's immersion in an atmosphere of sexlessness which, on her authority and that of others, obtained at that time in some circles of educated young people, or to the author's rebellion against the tyranny of romantic endings.

In terms of the structure of the novel, Rosamund's refusal to be loved is in key with the general insistence on the autonomy of the individual; but it is out of key with Rosamund's own urging that Verney lower his pride before his grandfather's need to be loved. At Verney's return to Rome after his grandfather's death, he has learned, that "all one's desires fail .... Yet one fell, not far, but on to the tableland of the second best. . . . It was a world of compensations. He had desired love, and had accepted instead friendship. . . . Most of [life] was a sort of *pis-aller*–making the best of things as they were. But it was a good *pis-aller*, after all" (387-88). The publisher of the novel refused, however, to share this stoical resignation; he could not allow an ending that would leave his readers romantically unsatisfied. He demanded that the novel end with an engagement, and "with set teeth" the young novelist wrote a one-page epilogue (*LL*, 16). It does nothing more, however, than leave the gate open.

There is, in fact, no adequate acknowledgment of sexual love in Rose Macaulay's novels until after World War I. A related aspect of her novels is her frequent use through her whole career of names that avoided identifying the character's sex–John, Louie, Cecil, Neville, Rome, Stanley, Evelyn, Denham, Carey, Julian, and Laurie are women; Laurie, "Margery," Kay, Jayne, and Vere are men–and in her last novel, written fifty years after *Abbots Verney*, she used no detail or pronoun that indicated which lover was of which sex until the death of one of them at the end. It will be noted that in this first novel the chief male characters have as their surname "Ruth."

The management of the ethical problem constitutes only part of the excellence of *Abbots Verney*, excellence that was recognized by reviewers in at least nine journals and newspapers. In a full-column article, the reviewer for the *Scotsman,* who referred to the new novelist R. Macaulay as "he," declared: "Almost every page is a sustained blaze of brilliant conversation. The wit is so keen that an occasional interval of commonplace dulness would be almost a relief." This praise is well deserved if one excepts the perhaps overly lengthy girlish discussions mentioned above. The opening scene in the Lake District, with ten-year-old Verney and his three boy cousins at the sheep-dog trials, laying bets, arguing, and encouraging the dogs in the shepherds' dialect, is a triumph of lively presentation. In Rome, when Verney is in disgrace because of his father's cheating, Lady Anstruther is telling Rosamund how embarrassed she was at having to cut him when she had met his eyes directly. Rosamund inquired calmly, "Why did you cut him, by the way?"

"Rosamund! Of course one must. *Everybody* knows about it, you know."
"Well, I don't see what that's got to do with it."
Lady Anstruther . . . did not want to be nasty, and no one could say she was a prude, but still, there were limits. When people–people's fathers, any how (and there was nothing to prove that it stopped at the father)–were dishonest–well, in short, they had overstepped the limits.
Rosamund, to whom limits were, as a rule, more or less slurred, differed on the subject. (179)

Here, as in all of Rose Macaulay's work, the presence of the "implied author" is strongly felt.[2] In fiction she follows Jane Austen and George Eliot in this respect. "The real pleasure of Rose Macaulay's novels," wrote one critic, "lies principally in the personality of their writer. . . . throughout her novels, we are conscious of a brisk and entertaining companion, who at intervals talks to us herself."[3]
Aphoristic passages frequently appear. The suspicion with which the Ruths view intellectual brilliance gives rise to this description of one of the characters: "She had been born and bred in a nursery which sharpens wits, and attaches to learning a weight which seems to many societies extravagantly dispropor-

tionate. From London to the country is a wide step, yet a bridge may cross the chasm; between country and University there is a great gulf fixed, and no bridge will cross it, for on neither side will a bridge be sought" (39).

The impatience with unthinking emotionalism that was to alarm some of Rose Macaulay's readers throughout her career brings about passages of revolt against conventional sentimentality. During the summer when Verney stays in Rome, he is reduced to making a bare living by painting the kind of pictures that tourists demand. One night he is walking through the streets of a slum when the moon comes out; looking upon the scene, he "saw" the only way in which reason and truth could paint it: the steep black streets, with the grotesque white streak of moonlight down the middle, where the great leaning houses let it in; the garish lights of the wine shops, and the lounging groups inside; two men who fought with each other," and "the moon leering down on it all like a great yellow cheese. It was more than ugly—it was ridiculous." He avoided the tourists' Piazza di Spagna and "returned along the shore of the river, listlessly watching the moon silver the stale foam on the caked, cut mud of the naked banks" (234-35).

The remarkable fusion of two elements not often found together, sensitivity of psychological perception and delight in wit, is achieved most memorably in Verney's long talk with Rosamund while convalescing. The conversation is brilliantly conceived: her elegant banter to cause him to realize that he is still far from well, the complications of civilized reserve on the part of both, Verney's sudden need for her to understand his relation to his family, her attempt to steer him to see by himself that he could afford the loss of pride in going home and that he should for old age's sake make the sacrifice. The *Scotsman* reviewer prophesied: "The book will make its mark." Certainly, it gave promise that the author would make hers.

II The Furnace

Rose Macaulay's second novel, *The Furnace*, which appeared in 1907, less than a year after *Abbots Verney*, is short and astonishing. It presents two bohemians, Betty and Tom Crevequer–

sad-eyed, stuttering, orphaned siblings just out of their teens–
who are living with innocent abandon in a pair of messy rooms
and in the noisy streets and restaurants of a Neapolitan slum. To
their slender remittance Tom adds his pay for making political
drawings for a yellow journal, while Betty occasionally performs
in a music hall; but their chief resource is carefree borrowing.
Their parents had been English gentlefolk; and, like the young
Macaulays, the boy and girl held fast to memories of a Golden
Age childhood gaily swimming and boating on the seashore at
Varazze, near Genoa.

A Jamesian[4] development is set in motion when the Crevequers
are discovered by some slight family acquiantances who are in
Naples for several months: a Mrs. Venables, who writes novels
and has come there "to absorb impressions" (21); her son Warren
and her niece Prudence, who paint; and her stolid schoolgirl
daughter Miranda. The Crevequers are pleased, for they genuine-
ly like people–and they enjoy the prospect of free meals. Intricate
interrelationships–involving good will, moral disapproval, gay
comradeship, intellectual bafflement, exploitation, the beginnings
of love, and frequent embarrassment–form, change, and re-form
between the imperceptive lady novelist, her self-regarding son,
and the sociable, inconscient Crevequers. Prudence alone (this
novel's cool, detached young woman) refuses to offer a friendship that would insult the recipient by being only fractional.

Mrs. Venables is kindly disposed toward the Crevequers; but,
lacking the intuition that would enable her to understand them,
she sets herself to studying them for copy. Being modern and
tolerant, she is disturbed to find herself shocked. She also organ-
izes neighborhood club meetings in order to pry into the souls
of "the People," their picturesque slum friends. Warren, despite
himself, continually seeks Betty's childishly gay company and
realizes that he is falling in love with her. Tom is drawn toward
Prudence, but she skillfully keeps their conversations impersonal.
Gradually, bit by bit, the Crevequers piece together a realization
of the Venables' unspoken reservations regarding them and begin
to feel shame.

Then, in the violent 1906 eruption of Vesuvius (an obvious
symbol of their moral ordeal, but not, at the date of writing, an

improbable event),[5] Betty, seeking Tom and finding him badly hurt, recognizes that they alone are each other's good—that only they can help each other, and that she cannot now, or perhaps ever, leave her brother in order to marry. The Crevequers decide to quit Naples and try to lead a better life back at Varazze. In a terminal discussion, after the manner of Ibsen, James, and Shaw, Prudence points out to Warren that, without relinquishing her austere ideals, she has gained greater understanding through the Crevequers. Although there is much about values that they don't know yet, they have at least "lived" (as Mrs. Venables has not) and "they have each other" (222). These siblings, three years before E. M. Forster's Schlegel sisters in *Howard End,* had found that, in his words, "the inner life had paid."[6]

The delicate Jamesian problems of the interrelationships of persons of different cultural standards and different degrees of perceptiveness are well conceived and managed. The reviewer in *Athenaeum* (November 30, 1907, 683) congratulated Rose Macaulay on her "extremely clever study of the clash of moral codes." He continued: "She [avoids] all false brilliancy and superfluous detail; and the interest of the book never flags." Her purpose was not, as in *Abbots Verney,* to satirize a powerful, complacent group, but to present and interpret likeable persons who are on the fringe of society.

The Creveqeurs are highly original characters. They are childlike, but their relationship is not at all sentimental; they vie with each other, tease, and scold. They find fun in repaying Mrs. Venables for their free meals by imaginatively supplying her with the kind of facts regarding folk customs that she so persistently demands. They are prophetic of later generations in claiming the right to continue, beyond adolescence, a frolicking life, on the seashore and in public places. "This feckless, guileless pair," as the *Spectator* reviewer (November 30, 1907, 872) termed the siblings—giving the novel the chief fiction review of the week—were to return to Rose Macaulay's readers five years later in *Views and Vagabonds.* So was Mrs. Venables, whom the reviewer recognizes, in spite of her devotion to art and to the soul, as a "prig" and a "philistine."

III   The Secret River

In 1909 there was published a small volume with four blue flowers on the cover venturing out from a vine that ran up the spine; it was Rose Macaulay's *The Secret River*, a work that defies classification. The frame is narrative, an extremely simplified presentation of discrete episodes in the life of a young poet. These episodes are interpreted through poetic impressions of real scenes and events and through symbolic ritualistic manifestations of nature. The work was an experiment of the sort that Virginia Woolf was to try, but with important differences, two decades later in *The Waves*. Unlike *The Waves*, *The Secret River* is not made up of expressionistic utterances by the characters but of narrative presentation by the author of transcendent experiences granted to, or won by, the young poet. Michael, as long as he is true to his gift, can hear, like Fiona Macleod, the voices of "the Hidden People" (second epigraph), and partake of ritualistic experiences afforded by various aspects of nature and by–as with the young Yeats–Beauty and the Rose.

The leading epigraph is a passage from Hermann Lotze: "Another world-order may exist here and now as an order of quite another kind without intruding itself or being noticeable in the course of the events of this world. On the other hand, we have no reason to regard these several world-orders as falling entirely outside one another: on the contrary, we must regard them as bound up together." Rose Macaulay explains her related concept of "the sacramental view of the world": for this, "two things are essential–the exquisite development of the senses, to apprehend fully the substances that strike on them, and the fine penetration of the spirit, to see the substances as translucent veils" (70). Michael had both of these gifts, but he had learn how to go beyond and pierce through these veils. Heading the various chapters are epigraphs drawn from Hilaire Belloc, Plato, John Fisher, Maurice Maeterlinck, William Butler Yeats, Sir Thomas Browne, the Earl of Surrey, Paul Verlaine, and John Bunyan–the young writer's wide reading had been very exciting to her–which deal with some aspects of this "sacramental view."

What story there is traces the life of the physically frail young poet from his idyllic twentieth birthday through his infatuation with a beautiful, shallow young woman who suddenly deserts him for his friend, and into a period of physical and moral break-down, from which he gradually recovers his delight in life. But then this young woman returns, and out of mistaken gallantry he consents to marry her; after the marriage, she sets about nagging him to pursue material success until he finally regains his contact with the unseen through death.

The opening sentences indicate the two types of imagery: "Mi-chael heard far off the thin, faint horns of the dawn, that pealed in reedy reiteration before the willows were grey. They were far off; but, nearer at hand, the thin pipings that the river people make . . . shrilled sweetly into his dreams . . ." (1). The "horns of the dawn" are in the "other world-order"; the "pipings" are actual. The moments of his life that are presented are experiences at the river; his birthday dawn; the noon of sexual promise, when, in Pre-Raphaelite symbolism, he was "led . . . at last, by mur-murous and humming ways, to the Rose at the World's End" (20); the night of the double treachery, when "evil things . . . came all about him, and lifted him on horrid wings" (32); the "rank days" of resultant dissipation, when "in and out of the heavy weeds live things crawled, flopping about the warm, stag-nant water, breaking the grey-green scum . . ." (46); the epi-phany of "the gate of the rose," when, recovering from his extreme illness, he experiences a sunset that makes the river a "path of flame . . . to a mystic altar" (68); the epiphany of death, when under the frosted willows, by "this lucid pallor of cold light," the icy river is a "pale path" and the keen, rarefied air promises spiri-tual freedom (81); April, when he regains his eager liveliness, and the river runs "full to the brim of buoyant, green water" (94); then the "old gold" summer that leads to his mistaken mar-riage (103).

Although Fiona Macleod's Hidden People and Yeats's Rose appear among the passages used for epigraphs, *The Secret River* is very different in tone from the yearning, somewhat Spasmodic passion of that Highland persona or the Twilight mythic passion of Yeats's early poems. For one thing, Michael is nearly childlike–resembling in this respect the characters of Maeterlinck from whom one epigraph is drawn and by whom Rose Macaulay said that the writers of her generation had been influenced.[7] Michael is also almost asexual–his infatuation is an artist's rather than a lover's. Then, whatever his transcendental powers, Michael is an actual Edwardian person; and his experiences take place at a river within an easy walk of his home. The various meteorological epiphanies themselves are not dreamy but definite. During his physical and spiritual convalescence, he sees at sunset "between the willows a sea of rose fire . . . ." It "glowed, a shining and living thing of translucent fire, blooming at Michael's feet, brimming with limpid flame from marge to marge, and the moving reeds made tiny eddies of liquid fire." Michael then recognizes it as "the mystic and illumined approach to the very gates of the temple . . . of the inviolate rose, which was beauty's self" (68-69).

The symbolic manifestations are imaginatively conceived and effectively represented in these set pieces, but this type of writing imposed narrow limits on the author's skills in reading life and interpreting it. Except in a few poems, she did not return to it. Better suited to her lively talent was the poetic description of actual nature. There is Michael's dawn swim; he lets the stream bear him "over the long, weedy strands that made way for him and slimily caressed him as he drifted through. His fingers dragged softly at them . . . and his feet pressed a water-way among the waving stalks. Willow leaves brushed his wet face . . . Michael slipped out of the shadow of the willow and leant his breast to the river and waded against it, and it eddied about his neck, and his feet caught it in the slimy roots of things. He paused to give good-morning to the bobbing lily-balls . . . slipping his fingers up juicy stalks . . ." (7-9). This passage is another of the many throughout Rose Macaulay's books that present her delight in swimming. Actual nature and the transcendental recognition of evil mingle in the river episode of "rank days": ". . . the gurgle of slimy mud yielding beneath their digging bodies was in his ears; . . . he covered his ears from the sounds he heard, but they pierced sibilantly through, the glutinuous gurglings and horrid whisperings. He buried his face in his hands, but the corrupt smell of old mud crawled through his fingers" (53-54).[8]

IV The Valley Captives

From 1901 to 1906, Rose Macaulay's father held a post in Wales at the University at Aberystwyth; and, when the brilliant young woman, her studies at Oxford completed, joined the family there in 1903, she felt herself in something of a state of exile. From this experience came *The Valley Captives* (1911), a novel whose bitterness sets it apart from all her other works. It concerns a morbidly sensitive and imaginative boy and his strong and protective sister, who are captives in a narrow Welsh community–and worse, captives in a household where conventional thought passes over into vulgarity and physical brutality.

Their father's retreat into a solely esthetic experience of life contrasts with the activity, crude but salutary, of the revivalists–a contrast similar to certain situations in E. M. Forster's *Where Angels Fear to Tread, The Longest Journey,* and *A Room with a View,* published within the preceding decade. These young Methodists are a new theme for Rose Macaulay, and the attempt to show their strengths, as well as their comic–and lamentable–crudities, is perhaps the most interesting aspect of this novel. As they sing their jingling hymns, the esthete "could not see the visible and audible commonness as a symbol that one might forget in what it stood for. He did not see the pathos and the pity and the courage of the weak, hopeful, unending fight against the enclosing walls–the courage that produced these tawdry weapons, saying, 'Here is all we have to fight with!' "(139.) Twenty three years later, Rose Macaulay was to treat this theme again in *Going Abroad.*

V Views and Vagabonds

Views and Vagabonds, published early in 1912, is the novel that announced Rose Macaulay's arrival at her own particular destination; it is completely "her type" of fiction. The crew of assorted characters engage in a running symposium–a "Menippean *cena,*" to use Northrop Frye's term[9]–over which the "implied author" (see ch. II, n. 2) presides with a brilliant irony that is by no means incompatible with sympathy. The action consists more or less equally in a series of confrontations and in the logical working out of a fey hypothesis–in this case, in relation to the egalitarian dilemma.

The hypothesis on which the story is based is that Benjamin

Bunter, a Cambridge graduate, the son of Lady Lettice and a Tory Member of Parliament, has "a quite unusual habit of converting theory into action" (26); so that, having renounced financial aid from his parents' unearned coal mine receipts and having become a blacksmith, he is now about to carry out his theory that "we should all marry the hardest workers we know" (33) by marrying a plain, silent, humorless, family-ridden girl three years his senior–mill-worker Louie Robinson.

Lady Lettice protests that he could fulfill the requirements of his theory with one of the "nice girls" who "work quite as hard, doing things at home, and going out, and all that. There's Doris Overton, now, always looking after her mother, who's so provoking, poor thing, and doing all the flowers herself, and seeing after everything, . . . besides all the golf she has to play, and debating societies and things . . ." (34-35). Benjie's older brother Hugh, a "detached" person, sees that Benjie's egalitarian theories are causing him to undervalue the individuals that they are intended to help. He observes: "He is making the only hopeless mistake– putting individuality underneath a cause" (38-39).

Cecil, Benjie's undergraduate cousin, has not seen this dilemma. With unquestioning enthusiasm, she is working for the establishment of the "equality idea"; busy as she is with her Cambridge studies, she has become a Fabian, and she finds time to bike out to the village after the marriage to guide Louie toward the progressive thinking appropriate to the women of today and to develop in her a taste for the new art. For Cecil holds that "you can't have a democracy till we can all come easily into other people's lives and interests." Benjie's undergraduate brother Jerry, "a poet, an actualist," scorns her idealism as an attempt to establish dull unanimity (46-49).

To provide a counterpoint to Benjie's earnestness, Rose Macaulay has brought from Italy those siblings of *The Furnace*, Betty and Tom Crevequer, who are now rambling about England in a pedlar's cart. To Benjie's principle "As long . . . as one doesn't let things get in the way of one's work–that's all that matters," they respond (but silently, for they are very kind): "as long . . . as you don't let your work get in the way of more things than need be–that was all that mattered" (15).

When Louie's baby dies shortly after birth because of her shift-

less father's stupid act, the kind Bunters invite their son and his
wife to visit them in London. The parents' attitude is complex:
since Louie is one of "the poor" and has had no education in art,
literature, and politics, Lady Lettice and Mr. Bunter attempt to
fill these lacunae and to make her more presentable. At the same
time, since there is at the moment something of a cult of "the
poor," they are pleased to have one of these to exhibit. Mrs.
Venables, the novelist in *The Furnace*, home now from Naples,
takes Louie around in order to study her reactions–for copy,
again. These she attempts to ascertain not by observation or intuition but by earnest questioning; after taking the mill-girl to St.
Paul's, she demands: "But did it *appeal* to you? Did it *stir* you?"
(111). Louie realizes that this relentless interrogation implies an
utter lack of concern for her as an individual: "Wi'out I was pore
. . . they's none of 'em care" (110). No one cares for what she really
feels–the loss of her baby; no one, not even her theorizing husband, offers her the personal love that would help heal her loss.
Some distraction would be afforded her if she were taken to the
fun-fair at the White City, as Hugh intelligently suggests; instead,
she is hustled off to more of the baffling plays, concerts, and
galleries.

With the acknowledgment of Louie's frustration, the novel
might seem to be moving toward the tragic. It recognizes the
tragic, but it remains comic; its focus is on the errors of the
upper-class characters rather than on the silent misery of Louie.
In novels by upper-class humanist intellectuals, characters like
Louie pose a problem.[10] From the start of her novel-writing, Rose
Macaulay had insisted that the individual be valued for what he
is and not as an example of some group to which one of his
characteristics might relegate him. Humanistic thought requires
that all persons be considered as ends in themselves, as ultimates;
in this respect it is non-hierarchical. But humanistic thought also
involves the concept of an essential human quality, or *virtù*
(intelligent comprehension, moral sense, or taste, or some combination of these), which distinguishes man from lower beings,
with individual human beings aligned in hierarchical order along
the scale of increasing degrees of this *virtù*. A philosophy of progress combines these two aspects of humanism: all individuals
should be given an equal "opportunity" to acquire more of the

essential *virtù*– to become more truly human. At any time, those who have progressed to a high point on the ladder have become, through having realized more of the human potentiality, more "real" than those still on the lower rungs or not climbing at all.

Novelists whose personal climate is that of wit, knowledge, and taste may find characters who share their intellectual world more "real" than those who do not. If the novelist's humanism is compulsive, he attempts to demonstrate certain values and to scrutinize current vogues and organized causes with regard to their promotion of these values. But, if he has also a highly developed sense of irony, he is struck by the indecency of the invasion practiced in trying to improve individuals. Finally, the irony turns itself back upon the novelist: unimproved individuals may seem to him too unreal for serious concern.

In *Views and Vagabonds* Rose Macaulay dealt for the first time (except for glimpses in *The Valley Captives*) with lower-class characters, and the plot of this novel involves a conflict between the humanistic desire for all human beings to become highly developed and the humanistic respect for individuals as they are. The lower-class characters are at a primitive stage of development–in regard to intelligence, or ethics, or esthetics, or to all three. The various uplifters fail, however, and even do harm, because of their lack of respect for individuality; and such failure in serious involvements implies elements of tragedy for both parties.

The only serious involvement in this novel is Benjie's and Louie's marriage, and its tragic aspect (together with Louie's bereavement) is acknowledged in brief glimpses: "And Louie clasped a rabbit, with her arms still empty and her eyes tired" (76). But, since the lower-class characters are persons of inadequate *virtù*, they apparently seemed to Rose Macaulay herself to verge upon the sub-human, the unreal. Except for these occasional glimpses into Louie's unhappiness, the encounters between the different classes are held to the level of comedy, and the uplifters themselves are reduced to comic simplicity so that there is less suggestion of three-dimensional persons engaged in shadow-boxing. The comic treatment, then, is a technique for coping formally with a quandary that certain characters inside the form

–Hugh and the curate Bob Traherne–refuse to allow to be solved so easily.

To Betty and Tom Crevequer–to whom a relative *ex machina* has just willed Merrilies End, a seaside estate in Suffolk!–everyone is an individual. They radiate an ambiance of sunny tolerance. At Merrilies, as Louie observes, "people . . . seemed to take each other for granted, and treated one person very much like another. That was restful" (130). These life-hungry siblings never tire of frolicking about–with their pet animals, their sailboat, their off-beat guests, and the needy persons whom they gladly support. One of the most delightful scenes in the book is a fantastic *agape* or love-feast–a garden party at Merrilies offered to all comers for the purpose of forwarding the election campaign of Benjie's father, although that Tory remains somewhat dubious about accepting this assistance, After the guests' opening moments of chilly categorizing–"the respectable . . . the disreputable . . ."– they abandon these generalities so wasteful of human values and mix and dance together as at some pagan festival (172).

Benjie is drawn by the Crevequers' naïve kindliness and verve; but his theories soon cause him to become indignant at their preference of fun to work and at their indiscriminate generosity, which is pauperizing the local irresponsibles. There is the ironic incident of Benjie's being knocked out while trying to shame these paupers and, upon regaining consciousness, finding that he is in bed in the Crevequers' house. Their kindly ministrations, which include bringing a basket of soft baby puppies to look at, he glumly refuses, since he disapproves of their principles.

During the period when Louie–disabused about Benjie's reason for marrying her and aware of the immaturity of his feelings–has chosen to live again with her own people, Cecil and her cousin Benjie spend the summer traveling about the countryside in the Crevequers' cart, trying to raise the taste of the villagers by showing them–and trying to sell them–sturdy, well-designed furniture that Benjie has made by hand and prints of Augustus John drawings. Knowing nothing of servantless homes, Cecil bothers the housewives on ironing day; her exhortations also are inconsiderately chosen: "Don't you *want* to have good things? I wish you'd begin and try and care about it" (196). In one village, Benjie, pointing out the cheap pretentiousness of a new row of jerry-built villas in pale yellow brick with "curiously battlemented porches," declares to their inhabitants: "I wouldn't stay in any of those houses for a moment if they were mine" and proclaims this ugliness "immoral". As a result he gets himself thoroughly thrashed (150-53). Cecil finds that the villagers take it for granted that she is Benjie's paramour.

While Benjie is still indignant at the childlike irresponsibility of the Crevequers, a fire (*ex machina*) suddenly consumes the house at Merrilies (uninsured, of course); and Benjie has his night of tragedy. Believing that the brother and sister are trapped in an atrocious death, he jerks himself free from the hindering police and rushes into the flaming hall in a desperate attempt to save them. Painfully burned and driven back, he experiences a profound epiphany; he realizes that these individuals Betty and Tom are what he loves most dearly in the world and that his theorizing has blinded him to real values. When the siblings reappear, safe and sound, he is ready to abandon his theories and projects and to join them in their gypsy cart.

But Betty's sense of individuals as ultimates leads him to recognize the claims of Louie as an individual–a wife whose devotion to himself he is, after all, responsible for. The renunciation scene is only sketched; any fully realized suffering at this point would lead too far from the comic norm. In any event, Betty would hardly have been available in a relation other than that of a comrade–she is too closely linked to her brother–and, furthermore, Benjie remains throughout the novel sexually immature. Permitted by the comic norm, and somewhat earlier in the story, came a Gilbert-and-Sullivan peripety involving the revelation to Benjie that he is actually a common man–the son of Lady Lettice's deceased sister by a common (and now thoroughly disreputable) sailor. Lady Lettice wants him to keep his discovery a secret, but Hugh points out that in becoming a born member of the working class Benjie "has achieved the ambition of a lifetime at last. You can't expect him to hide his glory" (243).

The book ends with another *agape*–of sorts. Cecil and Jerry come from Cambridge for Sunday tea at Benjie's and Louie's village home–shared by Benjie's hearty father, Louie's invalid sister, and little Stanley Wilfred (it had been Louie's turn for naming). Louie's parents also are guests, betraying as usual their place on the scale of human development. The house is a cheap, pretentious jerry-built villa of Louie's choice, named "Daisyville." On the walls Benjie's Augustus John prints and Louie's Coronation portraits mingle. In basic matters Benjie stands firm against her family's prejudices, but he cheerfully sacrifices the plays and concerts that used to delight him in order to accompany her to whist-drives and magic-lantern shows.

Obviously, this ending is ambivalent. Benjie has supposedly learned—for himself, and symbolically for the other uplifters—the lesson stated by the young mission-priest, Bob Traherne: "... you're trying to destroy personality. You're trying to enforce on people—on *people*, the genuine, live, sacred article—a system, a set of principles, a soulless code of life and art. You're trying to give them what you think they ought to like, not what they do like. You're despising personality" (220). A good lesson—but in only a few passages has the novelist brought herself to make such an inadequate person as Louie appear "live" and "sacred." Traherne is not opposed to attempting to change people; but his operant for change would be the inspiration of the Personality of God—Benjie and Cecil, he holds, should have tried to develop people from within. That a change toward greater *virtù* is highly to be desired is, in spite of the comic ambiance, the author's passionate belief; and Benjie's life at "Daisyville" is precariously balanced on the edge of the tragic. The novel might be said to have achieved a formal hilarity.

The "implied author" had teased Cecil because "there were so many problems in her difficult life. There are, if you are responsible for either the fitting in or the extermination of everyone you come across in an over-full world" (253). Perhaps the "implied author" is teasing the actual author. In the final pages, the troublesome underdeveloped have, for a time, disappeared as Cecil and Jerry, excitedly discussing poetry, drama, and natural beauty, bike back to Cambridge.

VI   The Lee Shore

In October of the same year, 1912, Rose Macaulay had a second book published, *The Lee Shore;* and this novel received the first prize—one thousand pounds—in a competition held by the publishing firm of Hodder and Stoughton.[11] The reviewer in *Spectator* made an interesting comment on this award. All too often, he observed, prizes go to a new novelist who thereafter never produces anything equal, or to someone who has been careful to follow the established conventions. This author, however,

> has already made her mark by at least three novels of quite uncommon merit—*Abbots Verney, The Furnace,* and *Views and Vagabonds.* But this is not all. *The Lee Shore* is emphatically not the sort of book that any well-conducted competitor would write who wanted to win the prize. . . . in an age when the worship of success is perhaps more pronounced than it has ever been before, it is unusual to find a book succeeding by its exceptionally sympathetic treatment of unsuccess, by its tender handling of ineffectual lives. . . . We congratulate the judges on their discernment and Miss Macaulay on her triumph. (CIX [October 26, 1912], 652)

If the term "Georgian" is used in the sense it has assumed since the publication, that same year, of *Georgian Poetry, 1911-1912, The Lee Shore,* is pre-eminently a "Georgian" novel. The sensitive young poet of *The Secret River* has been reconceived as the comically ill-starred Peter Margerison. Like the poet, Peter is physically fragile but game; he is devoted to visual beauty; and he loses his sweetheart to his friend. Peter's losses, however, cause him to lapse into no melodramatic end-of-the-century dissipation and breakdown. He sees his predestined role as comic: "Disasters seemed to crowd the roads on which he walked; so frequent were they and so tragic that life could scarcely be lived in sober earnest; it was, for Peter the comedian, a tragi-comic farce. Circumstances provided the tragedy and temperament the farce" (2). Without too much regret, he finds amusement and joy in the "Georgian" world of real matter and of actual people—the simple outdoor life of a lee shore.[12]

The opening episode typifies the entire story. The young schoolboy Peter, in agony from a shoulder dislocated in a football match, scarcely believes his good fortune in being noticed and aided by the godlike senior whom he worships, the school athlete Denis Urquhart. Denis knowledgeably sets the shoulder and binds it; but, pleased with his skill, he fails to notice that the shoulder has slipped out again. Despite his agony, Peter manages not to let Denis know: "Success was Urquhart's rôle; one did not willingly imagine him failing. If heroes fail, one must not let them know it" (5).

Peter and Denis are related, for Sylvia Hope, Peter's mother–and here is a typically fey situtation–had for a brief period had for her first husband Denis' handsome father, whose death soon terminated the passionate marriage, shortly whereafter she had married Mr. Margerison, a widower clergyman. The Urquharts are an aristocratic Berkshire family, headed by Lord Evelyn; the Hopes are Chelsea intellectuals, devoted to the arts, and to welcoming political refugees and supporting causes. Peter–everyone calls him "Margery"–has a genius for friendship: he finds interest in every sort of person, and he is exceedingly nice in his care not to obtrude his own concerns or to cause any discomfiture to others.

His pleasant undergraduate career at Cambridge is soon interrupted by his guardian's death, which leaves him without funds. Yearning to continue his connection with art, he finds that his connoisseurship is adequate to launch him on a career as art advisor to a wealthy but untrained Jew, Leslie. The two depart for Italy.

Peter is invited to walk across Tuscany by an ascetic friend, Rodney, an idealist and admirer of St. Francis. In terms of "the sacramental view of life" (ch. II, sec. 3) Peter is gifted with the necessary sensuous sensitivity; but he may perhaps never move to a more mystic phase. For him,

> ideas, the unseen spirits of life, were remote, neither questioned nor accepted, but simply in the background. In the foreground, for the moment, were a long white road running through a river valley, and little fortress cities cresting rocky hills, and the black notes of the cypresses striking on a background of silver olives. In these Peter believed; and he believed in blue Berovieri goblets, and Gobelin tapestries, and in a great many other things that he had seen and saw at this moment; he believed intensely, with a poignant vividness of delight, in all things visible. (56)

Both young men are contrasted with Denis, who chooses to race through the Tuscan dawn in a large, powerful motor car. This form of amusement results in the death of an aged woodgatherer, although Denis risks his own life to avoid hitting him.

Working for Leslie in Venice, Peter boards in a dilapidated *pensione* run by the motherly, slovenly Irish wife of his step-brother Hilary. The boarders are of the lowest level of English hangers-on in the world of art. Hilary, whose talent as a painter has proved insufficient, has undertaken to edit a connoisseurs' journal for Denis' art-loving uncle Lord Evelyn. Peter sees at once, however, that Hilary is receiving bribes for his critiques and splitting fees with certain dealers in purchasing fakes for his physically and mentally degenerating patron. Lord Evelyn has always been fond of Peter, and the young man tells his brother that this trickery must stop; but, realizing that Hilary and Peggy are in desperate economic need, he cannot condemn them in rigorous conventional fashion. Hilary does not, of course, desist; his practices are exposed; and Lord Evelyn–acutely hurt by what he paranoically supposes is Peter's complicity–requires both brothers to leave Venice and never again undertake a business connection with art. Peter's extreme code of loyalty prevents him from exculpating himself.

The Margerisons return to London, where their situation continues to deteriorate. Lucy Hope, Peter's loveable Chelsea cousin and playmate, his second self, has become infatuated with Denis and married him. A series of unlikely incidents–Peter's being begged by a dying woman to take care of her confused daughter; his listless marriage to this girl, who takes no interest in him; her departure with a flashy cad–is arranged, it would appear, to produce the baby Tommy, whose scenes with his delighted father are charming.

But now that Peter's connoisseurship has been rendered unusable, he is reduced to taking–and losing–a succession of unsuitable, wretchedly paid jobs; and in a world geared to success he is soon in extreme poverty. He had sold Leslie's parting gift, an exquisite medieval Venetian goblet, to give the money to Peggy–whom it helps, as usual, all too briefly. Meanwhile, Lucy has discovered how inadequately vital life is among Denis' set in Park Lane. Her family and friends in Chelsea "had had, mostly, a different kind of brain, a kind more restless and troublesome and untidy, and a different kind of wit, more pungent and ironic . . . ." In Park Lane she found "high living, plain thinking, agreeable manners and personal appearance, plenty of humour, enough ability to make a success of the business of living and not enough to agitate the brain, a light tread along a familiar and well-laid road, and a serene blindness to side-tracks and alleys not familiar nor well-laid and to those that walked thereon . . ." (229).

Herself "intensely alive," Lucy ponders the fact that "Denis hadn't any use for cranks. None of his set were socialists, vegetarians, Quakers, geniuses, anarchists, drunkards, poets, anti-breakfasters, or anti-hatters"; his set have neither the "romance" possible to plutocrats nor the dreams of the destitute, but "merely prosperity, which has fewer possibilities." And Rose Macaulay the essayist inserts at this point a critique of socialism, which eliminates these fruitful extremes and offers instead "the prosperous; the comfortable; the serenely satisfied; the sanely reasonable . . . the monotonous external adequacy that touches no man's inner needs, the lifeless rigour of a superintended well-being" (229-30). Denis, a serenely satisfied Conservative, finds socialism "rot"; he fails to see the parallel. Becoming more and more congealed in convention, Denis refuses to initiate a renewal of his friendship with Peter. Lucy, meeting Peter in a damp, fragrant beech wood on an April morning—the conventional location is delightfully fresh in this presentation—offers to go away with him, and he decides that he too, and Tommy, should finally "have."

But at this point Rodney, the ascetic, preaches Peter a sermon. He warns him that he would be false to his own nature if he deserted "the camp of the Have-Nots." To the "pleasant cheerfulness" of Denis' set, Peter should prefer "the gaiety, in the teeth of circumstances, of St. Francis and his paupers, who have nothing and yet possess all things" (289-91). Rodney also points out that Peter's long devotion to Denis would prevent him from ever being happy again if he eloped; personal loyalty is basic to Peter's way of living, if not to Denis'. Miserably, Peter agrees. The morning brings a renunciatory letter from Lucy with the same recognition of the barrier of Peter's love for Denis.

The next spring Peter and Tommy are living in that Macaulay haven, Varazze: "There is a shore along which the world flowers, one long sweet garden strip, between the olive-grey hills and the very blue sea" (297). Peter, it will be observed, is permitted to enjoy anything that nature freely gives; he need not–like Hardy's Tess–serve his term as a "Have-Not" in some gratuitously bleak landscape. On this shore Peter sells the embroideries that he makes and exchanges kindnesses with the villagers and nomadic pedlars. Here Lord Evelyn discovers him, makes up with him, and asks him to live with him for the short time he has left. But Peter feels he must not accept. Rose Macaulay takes care, however, to leave the future open for Peter and for Tommy. Life on "the lee shore" is not a sociological solution or a mystic neverland but a frame of mind. Only with "the gaiety of the saints" can one rightly cope with life, this *"pis-aller,"* and be generous-minded with one's brothers.

The Lee Shore is a curious work. In the multiplicity of characters and incidents only Peter is developed as a first-plane figure; his delicacy, pluck, and sense of his own comedy are delightful. He is a "created," not an observed character, and he is unforgettable. But the plot requires of him–and of Lucy–marital involvements that are inappropriate to their conception; they make charming playmates, but not lovers–nor spouses in their respective marriages. They seem to have resulted from that cult of the childlike–that protest against sophistication and mechanization–that gave rise to Maeterlinck's *L'Oiseau Bleu.* In *Views and Vagabonds,* Cecil (whose taste was good) praised this play–performed at the Haymarket in 1909–whose chief characters, a brother and sister, look through a window at the high living of the rich but find happiness in their own simple cottage. Peter's boyish devotion to Denis–his "squandering" of affection on that content, prosperous young man–is a datum that remains unanalyzed though it shares the importance of his love of beauty as a motivating factor (47).

The childlike level of Peter and Lucy dominates the book. At a Sunday tea at the Hopes', when Lucy's father and older sister offer hospitality to refugee artists, intellectuals, and revolutionists from the Continent, these guests appear to Lucy and Peter as unwashed, ill-barbered children would to a carefully tended child. Lucy's solution of the refugees' problems is rather facile (although she avoids the self-deception of Mrs. Venables and the Bunters of *Views and Vagabonds*): "Why can't they be happy?

There are so many nice things all about. 'Tis such *waste*" (48).
But the best aspects of the plot and style constitute a lyric of
Peter's unique, springtime consciousness.

The writing is managed with great skill. Fragments suggest so
effectively that the reader does not realize how brief they are.
Peter goes to say goodbye to the Hopes before leaving for Italy,
and in three pages (with large type) there are vividly presented
a conversation between Denis and Lucy involving an invitation
to herself and her father to accompany him on a motor trip to
Italy, her reluctant refusal, a discussion between Peter and Lucy
about several things including her sister's forthcoming marriage,
a flashback to a conversation between Peter and his employer
Leslie, and Peter's departure for Italy and arrival there. The
author's versatility encompasses the very different colloquial
styles of the many characters. And the "implied author's" master-
ly use of epigrammatic and of sinuous sentences suggests the
spiritual sturdiness of her young hero and his delicate tact.

VII The Making of a Bigot

In an essay, "Coming to London," written in 1957 for John Lehmann's collection on this subject,[13] Rose Macaulay told how she
gradually became a member of the intellectual and artistic world
of pre-World War I London. In the last years of King Edward's
reign and the beginning of King Geoge V's "I sometimes went up
[from Cambridge] to meet Rupert [Brooke, an "old friend of
ours"] for lunch or dinner and plays, and his friends, who were
apt to be poets, such as Edward Thomas and Wilfred Gibson and
Ralph Hodgson and others, sometimes came to lunch too, usually
at the Moulin d'Or." She and Brooke had won a number of prizes
from the *Westminster Gazette* in competitions on "problems" involving writing poems (see ch. III, sec. 1); and between 1910 and
1912 she met the editor of that section, Naomi Royde-Smith, a
brilliant talker and "the centre of a lively and able circle of friends.
... With her I met, in this pre-war golden age, a number of people
who seemed to me, an innocent from the Cam, to be more spark-
lingly alive than any in my home world." Then "before the end
of 1913 my uncle gave me a flat . . . where I used to spend part
of each week. I had a small house-warming party there; I forget

exactly who came, but certainly W. J. de la Mare did, and Naomi Royde-Smith . . . and Rupert . . . and some other poets" (158-64). The year 1913 she later regarded as her *Annus Mirabilis* (*L*, 17).

Out of this near-chaos of stimuli came her next work of fiction, *The Making of a Bigot*, published early in 1914. It resembles *Views and Vagabonds* in being based on a Gilbert-and-Sullivan hypothesis–that there can exist a hero who incarnates some logical position–but the wit is more economically achieved than in the earlier novel. In *The Lee Shore* Peter had said–of politicians– "I rather like both sides. . . . They're both so keen, and so sure they're right" (163); and, of his baby's baptism, "Thomas . . . can be anything he likes that's nice. As long as he's not a bigot. I won't have him refusing to go into one sort of church because he prefers another; he musn't ever acquire the rejecting habit" (227). Eddy, the young Cambridge graduate who is the hero of this next book, has "a receptive mind." When asked "Are you a–," he answers at once, "Yes, I'm everything of that sort." And he adds that his questioner "won't be able to think of anything I'm not" (10-11). "Surely," he comments, "shouldn't one encourage everything?" His father wants him to follow the family tradition and take Orders. In Eddy's mind "the question was, could one select some one thing to be, clergyman or anything else, unless one was very sure that it implied no negations, no exclusions of the other angles?" (17). And so, accepting, this amiable young man pursues his investigation of life through this *Bildungsroman* (see ch. II, sec. 1) where realism–sometimes tragic–and fey comedy both have a part.

At first Eddy works in a Church of England settlement in a slum. Here he finds that the senior and junior curates and the young laymen all have differing allegiances and deplore each other's views; their interplay is worked out in a comic geometry. His nervous agnostic friend, Arnold, deplores the lot of them and introduces Eddy to a clutch of progressive young people: a jolly "militant" suffragette[14] and a detached other-worldly artist–young gentlewomen who elect to live away from their families in a one-room apartment in Blackfriars; a married couple, the Le Moines, now separated but still friendly–she, a sensitive violinist, and he, an avant-garde playwright; and their friends, who, according to the junior curate, are "well, rather rotters, you know. Look like artists, or Fabians, without collars, and so on"(33).

When Eddy is often absent from the settlement at theater parties, at concerts, and on cross-country Sunday walks with these
talented young people, his vicar warns him that he cannot "fit it
all in" (74). At Eddy's invitation, Eileen Le Moine has delighted
the club youths with her music, which is a revelation to them;
but the vicar rules out any more visits, for her friendship with
Datcherd–a selfless agnostic social reformer separated from his
frivolous wife–although it is innocent, would give scandal: ". . . no
man and woman are 'great friends' in the eyes of poor people;
they're something quite different. . . . It starts talk" (76). Eddy
finally realizes that he cannot accept the limitations that this work
imposes.

Desiring that all the people he is fond of should know and like
each other, he invites several of the young Londoners to spend
New Year's with his parents in the cathedral town where his
father is dean. This house-party–this "Menippean *cena*" (see ch.
II, n. 9)–generates a series of frustrating encounters as these two
parties of civilized, well-disposed people become increasingly
aware of their differing frames of reference. The author takes the
occasion to make some good analyses of unfair forms of argument–appeals from the esthetic matter under discussion to moral
or sentimental standards which cannot be answered without
rudeness and so leave a courteous discutant without a response,
and the adducing of obscure evidence which is never clearly
brought forth (because there are young girls present). There are
several illustrations of faulty judging of persons resulting from
inadequate imaginative powers.

Shortly afterwards, asked to help at Datcherd's agnostic Social-
ist settlement while the exhausted reformer takes a rest-cure,
Eddy repeats his earlier permissiveness, inviting young church-
men and politicians of various persuasions to speak. Hearing of
this well-meant program, Datcherd cuts short his rest and returns,
haggard with anxiety.

Eileen's relation to Datcherd is of great interest as being the
first portrayal by Rose Macaulay of passionate sexual love; and,
furthermore, it is a powerful portrayal. The couple had denied
themselves the consummation of their love because it would give
scandal and consequently harm the youth-club work to which

Datcherd is devoting his life. Only when his health has broken down and death is certain to come soon does Eileen go away with him for the pitifully short period that he has left. Eileen has been presented as an extraordinarily fine young woman; and, as she and Datcherd have long since been dissociated from their marriage partners, the adultery involves no disloyalty. When Eileen returns to London, however, heartsick after Datcherd's untimely death, she is generally ostracized.

Some avoid her because, without analyzing it, they list her action as morally wrong; others, however, coolly view it in terms of an amoral but rigid social code and judge that she has put herself "beyond the pale." With these latter, neither Eddy nor his creator has any patience. The former class includes simple-hearted Molly, the daughter of a neighboring "county" family, to whom Eddy has become engaged. He pleads with her to see his friends as he does: "Just know the people, and you won't be able to help caring for them. People are like that—so much more alive and important than what they think or do, that none of that seems to matter" (227). She cannot think this way, and breaks the engagement. Arnold, by no means condemning Eileen, holds that the action was wrong for a reason apparently shared by the author: ". . . it was giving rein to individual desire at the expense of the violation of a system which on the whole, however roughly and crudely, made for civilisation, virtue, and intellectual and moral progress; . . . it was, in short, a step backwards into savagery, a giving up of ground gained" (223).

During the house-party at the deanery, the author has the young guests mention *The English Review*—which had started publication in 1908 and had included the leading Edwardian writers, but which was not among the periodicals taken by the dean—and the *Blue Review*, which had just been launched in 1913, with a dinner at the Cheshire Cheese, by Middleton Murry and Katherine Mansfield (*TGLS*, 258). "One is sure," wrote a reviewer, "that the characters are drawn from life, as most of the places certainly are . . . . The artistic set of London which fluctuates between Chelsea and Soho is well described" (*Saturday Review*, XVII [March 21, 1914], viii).

Arnold and Eddy begin publishing a magazine, *Unity*, in which opposing views are expressed by prominent specialists (the persons named are actual contemporaries), but the venture fails. Shortly after, during the violence that attends the 1913 dock strike, Arnold, on a visit to the scene, rather improbably jumps up on a cart and expresses his opinion with his usual scorn; the angry men drag him down and kill him. Eddy, standing near by, is wounded by partisans of both sides—rejected, as it were, for being of no use to either. While he is convalescing, Eileen insists upon sacrificing her friendship with him in order that his engagement with Molly—another *pis-aller*—may be resumed. For the sake of Molly and the world, then, he sets out to perfect his bigotry.

At the end, the book resumes its fey tone. The night before his marriage Eddy gives a dinner party which, like the lawn party in *Views and Vagabonds,* includes all his differing friends. For one glorious evening they chat together, and the opposites appreciate each other. After they have departed—gone their centrifugal ways—Eddy sits down "to decide his opinions," aided by a pack of cards. He pairs organizations that would strike "the ordinary person as incompatible" and rejects one. When he makes choices, they are to the left; in cases where he has no preferences, he cuts the cards. By dawn he is ready: "What a lot he would be able to accomplish, now that he was going to see one angle only of life and believe in it so exclusively that he would think it the whole." He cheats a little, allowing himself to dream of a time when all his friends would truly accept each other:

> . . . his friendships weren't, couldn't be, part of the price he had to pay for his marriage, or even for his bigotry. With a determined hand he painted them into the picture, and produced a surprising, crowded jumble of visitors in the little house—artists, colonels, journalists, civil servants, poets, members of Parliament, settlement workers, actors, and clergymen. . . . He must remember, of course, that he disliked Conservatism, Atheism, and Individualism; but that, he thought, need be no barrier between him and the holders of these unfortunate views. And any surprisingness, any lack of realism, in the picture he had painted, he was firmly blind to.

And, as he continues, his thought merges into the author's teasing commentary—"gradually he would become the Complete Bigot. . . . Then and only then, when, for him, many-faced Truth had resolved itself into one, when he should see but little here below but see that little clear . . . then and only then would he be able to set to work and get something done." And, playing the idea like a trout through another paragraph, the novelist leaves him "to start betimes upon so strenuous a career" (295-301).

The author grants that to achieve in this world one must limit his field of practice, and that the strife of opposing bigots keeps human efforts taut and at the ready. But Eddy's myriad devotions point out equal claims on the other side: his acceptance of causes reminds the reader that every cause appears sensible from some human point of view; his tolerance–his affection–for those holding widely differing views serves to plead against the human waste resulting from the stupidity of bigotry. An extension of this idea to the competing potentialities within the individual is among the speculations in *What Not* (1919).

VIII   Non-Combatants and Others

When World War I broke out, Rose Macaulay was dividing her time between her little flat in London and her family's home near Cambridge. She worked in Cambridgeshire for short while as an amateur nurse in the Voluntary Aid Detachment and then as a land-girl; but, at her father's death in 1915, she entered upon work more suitable to her mind and physical strength with a post in the War Office. In 1916 she published *Non-Combatants and Others*.

Although the chief characters are sensitively and vividly presented, and there are many amusing scenes of satire that sketch in the lesser characters, *Non-Combatants* belongs to the genre of serious journalism as much as to that of the novel; one handbook lists it, in fact, under "Essays." Its purpose is obviously to awaken readers to the psychological damage wrought by war, to set forth judgments regarding various phases of "war work" and wartime thinking, and to lead people of good will toward effective means for achieving peace and preventing future wars.

In the main line of the plot, Alix, the daughter of a Polish political martyr and an Englishwoman, Daphne, who combines great intelligence and charm in her world-wide campaign for the Society for Promoting Permanent Peace, is sickly and so over-sensitive that she cannot bear to contemplate the War. While her girl cousins do VAD work or drive ambulances, she is sent to live in a London suburb with some distant family connections at their cottage, "Violette." Mrs. Frampton and her daughters, Kate and Evie, belong to the unthinking level of the middle class. Through the conversations of their group, the novelist points up the irrationality that sways this large class; Alix wonders: "Were discussions at Violette, discussions in all the thousands of Violettes, always like this? Not argument, not ideas, not facts. Merely statements, quotations rather, of hackneyed and outworn sentiments, prejudices second hand, yet indomitable, unassailable, undying, and the relation of stories, without relevance or force . . ." (92-93).

Jarred out of her withdrawal by the suicide, at the front, of her brother, Alix finds her mind partly convinced by her mother's arguments for active pacifism; her imagination, too, is moved by a young High Church curate's explanation of the Church's effort against war. At the end, she decides that she, too, must act, must do "something *against* war . . . . Something to fight it, and prevent it coming again" (223).

To Daphne, an extraordinarily attractive woman, the author has assigned the role of setting forth some of the most soundly conceived programs for peace that were being proposed by various groups during World War I. In Cambridgeshire, she goes about the countryside starting village study circles. Democracies, she points out, are not inherently peaceful and intelligent; people must "*make*" them so "by a long and difficult education." They must learn not to "lump other people together in masses and groups, setting one group against another, when really people are individual temperaments and brains and souls, and unclassifiable" (258-59). It is not enough to desire general disarmament; the practical means for attaining it must be studied. Some of these views are very cleverly and effectively presented as intercalated observations during a series of typically inept speeches by well-meaning pacifists. Daphne travels about conferring with the governments of neutral nations, working toward "Continuous Mediation without Armistice"—"a continuous conference of the neutral nations, to convey the ever-changing desires of the belligerents to one another, to inquire into the principles of international justice and permanent peace underlying them, to discuss, to air proposals, to suggest, to promote understanding between belligerents" (265-66).

Through her, a great many pieces of practical wisdom are offered to the reader, as when she tells Alix that she must not be so fastidious as to refrain from working for causes because she dislikes some of the co-workers. And "it's quite time you learnt that there's no fighting with whole truths in this life, . . . all we can do is to seize fragments of truth where we find them, and use them as best we can" (270).

One unusual aspect of this book among publications early during the war is its insistence on the psychological damage being wrought. The VAD cousin says of the soldiers: "After all, what they can bear to go through, we ought to be able to hear about." But Alix, who had witnessed the cousin's brother, then on leave, having a hideous nightmare, thinks to herself: "but they can't, they can't, they can't"; and "we can't, we can't, we can't" (29-30). Mrs. Frampton fails to recognize cause and effect in the troublesome, quarrelsome ways of the Belgian refugees: "To think of them behaving like that, after all they've been through" (50).

The exposure of the clichés, misinformation, and jubilant non sequiturs that comprise the thinking of the class typified by "Violette" is carried out with brilliant satirical techniques; but it is interspersed rather too often by irrelevant comments on linguistic differences between the classes and on the mediocre taste found in this environment.

Alix' surviving brother deplores the jingoistic journalism and the loose talk about atrocities and spy scares. As for war poetry, he comments that so far most of it is "a flood of cheap heroics and commonplace patriotic claptrap—"it's swept slobbering all over us . . . ." The war has filled too many writers "with vim and banal joy" (71-73). An important theme—loosely relevant—is Alix' trying out of various types of churches and considering the concept of God and of man's relation to God that each implies. This was to reappear with increasing frequency in Rose Macaulay's writing, especially in the 1930's and after World War II.

CHAPTER 3

Poems, 1914 and 1919

I The Two Blind Countries

IN the spring of 1919 Edward Marsh, assembling poems for a
fourth volume of *Georgian Poetry*, wished to delay no longer
in including some work by a woman poet. When three of his
advisors argued for their favorites–Charlotte Mew, Edith Sitwell,
and Rose Macaulay–he disappointed them all by choosing Frede-
gond Shove. Rose Macaulay's advocate, who protested Marsh's
choice, found Mrs. Shove's work "neither strong enough nor, especially, individual enough" (Ross, 203 [see ch. II, n. 9]).

Individuality was a quality that had immediately struck the
reviewers when Rose Macaulay's first collection, *The Two Blind
Countries*, appeared in April, 1914. Harold Munro's review, "An
Interesting Woman-Poet," began: "The poetry of Rose Macaulay,
which may have been noticed by those who read the *Westminster*
and the *Spectator* (her six novels are known to a considerable
public) comes to us in its collected form as a lovely surprise; her
first book is one which I find it difficult to describe in the restrained manner necessary in such a composition as this Chronicle"
(*Poetry and Drama*, II [June, 1914] 180-81). He found the collection "peculiarly pleasant and stimulating." The reviewer in
Spectator declared:

> Miss Rose Macaulay in her slim book of verses, *The Two Blind
> Countries*, seeks a different prize from most poets. It is magic that
> she would capture–not the common magic of poetry, which is
> only a rarefied beauty, but that authentic thing which gives one a
> strange thrill and shudder and makes the solid earth seem an un-
> substantial vapour. It is homely magic, too, springing out of com-
> mon incidents, for the other world is always there, with only a
> gossamer veil between its strangeness and our high noontide. . . .
> In these verses we have all the gusto of ordinary life, and a sin-

gular gift of sharp delineation, but their charm is the imminence
of "the dream country" . . . (XIII [July 11, 1914] 58).

This collection of thirty-three poems was followed in October,
1919, by *Three Days*, a collection of twenty-nine. Six years later
an untitled and undated selection of twenty-two poems from these
two books appeared as number six in the Second Series of *The
Augustan Books of English Poetry* (with an introduction by Humbert Wolfe [London, *ca*. 1925]). Other poets republished in this
series were John Donne, George Herbert, Francis Thompson, W.
B. Yeats, Harold Monro, and Arthur Waley. Although Rose Macaulay continued to write and publish occasional poems, she did
not collect them.

In his introduction to the *Augustan* selection, Humbert Wolfe
observed:

> Miss Rose Macaulay has a wide and deserved reputation as a nov-
> elist. The popular imagination has tended to isolate as her leading
> characteristic wit, and with justice. Because the wit in her writing
> represents in part the balance of her artistic vision, and in part the
> sudden illuminations cast by that vision, as actual as the beams of
> a dark lantern. The dark lantern is a true image to apply to her
> work, because those who like it best have always been aware of
> something held back, some power or quality in reserve. They have
> been convinced that some day she will bring that asset into play,
> and they believe that it will prove to have in it as much of tears
> as of laughter. (iii)

The title of *The Two Blind Countries* is drawn from a line in
the introductory poem, "The Alien":

> On either side of a gray barrier
> The two blind countries lie;
> But he knew not which held him prisoner,
> Nor yet know I.

This passage recalls the chief epigraph to *The Secret River*—on the
coexistence of "several world-orders." In these poems, the other
orders—those outside "this world" of Cambridge civilization—are
the sinister passions, the dead, the vast geological epochs, the

inscrutable mind of God, and nothingness. Glimpses of these other states may hearten, confuse, or numb the seer. But she will not pay the homage of a portentous style, nor give way to self-pity. The readers of *Views and Vagabonds* and *The Lee Shore* would immediately have recognized the author of "Trinity Sunday":

> As I walked in Petty Cury on Trinity Day,
>   While the cuckoos in the fields did shout,
> Right through the city stole the breath of the may,
>   And the scarlet doctors all about
>
> Lifted up their heads to snuff at the breeze,
>   And forgot they were bound for Great St. Mary's
> To listen to a sermon from the Master of Caius,
>   And "How balmy," they said, "the air is!"
>
> And balmy it was; and the sweet bells rocking
>   Shook it till it rent in two
> And fell, a torn veil; and like maniacs mocking
>   The wild things from without peered through.
>
> Wild wet things that swam in King's Parade
>   The days it was a marshy fen,
> Through the rent veil they did sprawl and wade
>   Blind bog-beasts and Ugrian men.
>
> And the city was not. (For cities are wrought
>   Of the stuff of the world's live brain.
> Cities are thin veils, woven of thought,
>   And thought, breaking, rends them in twain.)
>
> And fens were not. (For fens are dreams
>   Dreamt by a race long dead;
> And the earth is naught, and the sun but seems:
>   And so those who know have said.)
>
> So veil beyond veil illimitably lifted:
>   And I saw the world's naked face,
> Before, reeling and baffled and blind, I drifted
>   Back within the bounds of space.
>
>   *   *   *   *
>
> I have forgot the unforgettable.
>   All of honey and milk the air is.
> God send I do forget. . . . The merry winds swell
>   In the scarlet gowns bound for St. Mary's.

This poem is certainly (despite overly conventional diction in stanza five) one of the outstanding poems of the "Georgians." Of her vision the *Times Literary Supplement* reviewer said: "Almost everything 'ordinary' in this book has a crooked, uncertain look. We know that the world is imperceptibly tumbling into ruin –which is only exaggerated change" (April 9, 1914, p. 174).

Harold Monro observed: "She writes in the Cambridge manner; she is of the school of Rupert Brooke and Frances Cornford." This "manner" was a controlled witty style, conveying a line of thought that rebels against traditional reverences and recognizes the irony of man's plight. The speaker in "Trinity Sunday" refuses reverence to the Day, the doctors, the church building, and the Master of Caius, choosing a comic doggerel with hovering accent that reduces the doctors to complacent animals, who "snuff." But the speaker's daring glance has taken her too far beyond civilization's screens; eager curiosity, a sense of triumph over the conventional and material, give way to horror at the final vision of nothingness. Hastily she retreats to a state of consciousness that human beings can endure.

In the first years of this century English poetry badly needed, among other things, new rhythmic modes–a need that Walter de la Mare, W. B. Yeats, the Imagists, T. S. Eliot—and, posthumously, Gerard Manley Hopkins–variously filled. Rose Macaulay's experimentation was chiefly with the element of rhythm. Her extraordinary mastery of this element was being demonstrated in the prose of her novels. Harold Monro said in his review: "I should think Miss Macaulay has little aptitude for writing in free verse; she is evidently helped by rhyme and rule . . . ." He declared: "Her technique is not particularly strong: one of its few surprises consisting in crowded syllables, protracted rhythm and delayed stresses often in the penultimate lines of stanzas where an ordinary iambic line might have been expected, imitative, doubtless unconsciously, of Mr. de la Mare."

Although Rose Macaulay and Walter de la Mare were both experimenting with syncopated counterpointing–anticipations and delayed stresses–he appears to have aimed primarily at a flowing musical continuity, while she seems to have actively avoided such an effect. Edward Thomas found that "the majority" of her poems "are decidedly more intellectual and less sensuous than Mr. de la

Mare's best work" (*Bookman, XLVI* [September, 1914], 251). The lines of "Trinity Sunday" with their crowded syllables and their syncopations require the reader to struggle with each line and to collaborate in the satirical process as he reads. In "Keyless," a mood poem, the groping rhythm conveys the thought exactly:

> Like a lost child my strayed soul drifted
> Back from the lit, intelligible ways
> Into the old, dim, environing maze
> Where remote passions and shadows shifted.

As the *Times Literary Supplement* reviewer observed, "The technique of her drifting, hinting, almost furtive verse is exceedingly interesting . . . ."

The ending of this poem shares one of De la Mare's techniques, that of clustered stresses, as the dreamer is brought home: "Sudden in the paddock the old cock crew,/ As if a key shrieked in a lock grown rusty." "The Losers," a poem related to *The Lee Shore*, modifies the stanza of Oscar Wilde's "The Ballad of Reading Gaol" to give an effect of exhaustion—

> The soft dust on the by-roads
>   Is shaken and stirred
> By the shuffling feet of a listless folk.
>   But no sound is heard,
> For they slouch along, a tired trail,
>   With never a song or word. —

and a questioning of human identity: "The gray dust on the by-roads/ Is shuffled and blurred . . ."/ making "a quiet sound" ". . . as if/ A thousand sleepers stirred."

Remnants of the late Pre-Raphaelite style are found in several poems in this collection. The competitions in the *Saturday Westminster Gazette* in the preceding decade had called for the writing of ballades, sonnets, sestinas, and terza rima; and in Rose Macaulay's winners she uses the medieval, Oriental, and Celtic imagery that had come to be associated with these forms[1] "Peace and the Builder," a 1907 sonnet republished in *The Two Blind Countries,* used the images "a house of ivory," "cedar-wood," "myrrh," and "wind-riven years," "dim slope," "pale wanderer." "Hands," a poem of resignation, is in terza rima; this form is tightened by riming each group of two tercets on the same rimes and loosened by running-over several of the tercets. The thought is a variant on the traditional theme of comfort from the physical touch of the vines, flowers, and winds–a concept that reappears in a more sophisticated development in the dedicatory poem of *Three Days.* "A Ligurian Valentine" is a fresh little album piece in the form of a villanelle, recalling the poet's delight in her childhood on the Italian Riviera. "Turning Back," on the "Losers" theme, is a sestina; it remains something of an exercise–with, however, this striking passage: "Oh mystery/ Of use that drives us crosswise to our will . . . ." "The New Year" and "The Old Year" are rondeaux. Some of these poems retain a diction that includes such words as "thee," "O," and "yea"; there is talk of "beauty" and "the gods"; and allegory is frequent.

Among other allegorical poems is "The City on the Lee Shore," another "Losers" poem; the thought is led along a path of subtle rhythms:

> Down the blue buoyant shipways adventure no more,
> For the ports of desire are remote and hidden;
> Drop hope, the peaceless pilot, and drive storm-ridden
> Where winds and tides make an end, upon the lee shore.

For all the restless variety in the movement, each of the twenty lines is of exactly twelve syllables, a fact of which the reader is vaguely conscious, and which contributes to the sense of security in resignation. The traditional imagery develops unexpected strength in the third line of the quoted quatrain, and in a "newer" line: "And pile their wrecked cargoes to make a little fire."

"Saint Mark's Day," a comic poem, takes its place in a large body of Georgian verse involving the life of the people. It is composed in a doggerel development of ballad stanza, with a touch of dialect. A spiteful couple tell Dolly that the visions of St. Mark's Eve have shown that she will die before the year is out:

> But they and their lie, they've made Dolly cry;
> I heard her in the yard just now,

As she hung out the clothes for the west wind to dry,
Sobbing so she didn't heed how

The blown apple-bough set the light line swinging
Up and down, and tossed her dad's shirt
Over the blackthorn hedge . . . .

The *Spectator* reviewer found Rose Macaulay's "magic" to be "most potent" when she "weaves her spell about something home-ly or grotesque," and he referred at this point specifically to "Three." Out in the hot chalk hills beyond Cambridge, the speaker is reading and contemplating her uninteresting picnic food when she gradually becomes aware of a "stealthy," "evil" life throbbing nearby. The young lady becomes needy in contrast with the self-sufficient being who is revealed–a "satyr-king" of a tramp:

He had a beard like a dandelion,
    And I had none;
He had tea in a beer-bottle,
    Warm with the sun;
He had pie in a paper bag,
    Not yet begun.

In "The Tramps' Highway" the tramp is lulled by the singing telegraph wire: "In the boot-strewn ditch he will perhaps sleep long;/ Among jampots he may sleep deep."

The *Times Literary Supplement* and *Bookman* reviewers quoted parts of "The Thief," a poem in which eerie aspects of early dawn outside a house in a garden mingle with luscious and pungent imagery as a mysterious thief eats fruit; the poem was included in W. H. Davies' anthology, *Shorter Lyrics of the Twentieth Century* (London, 1922). "Cards" is perhaps the most formally suc-cessful of the poems; a sonnet, it profits from its compactness, although the rhythms are so delicately varied that one might not be aware of its decasyllables and rime-scheme; eight of its lines open with spondees, and eight are enjambed. During an evening card-game, a lover fights against the evil things of night that sidle behind the beloved's chair; the poem ends with a telling line: "You said, 'Our game,' more truly than you knew."

The first of the "Two Hymns for St. Andrew's Day" is an extraordinary poem in eight-foot lines. This verse-form is soon recognized as a strong-swinging version of "In Memoriam" stanza arranged in two lines instead of four; Oscar Wilde has used it in his bizarre poem, "The Sphinx." From a Christopher Smart world come the voices of missionaries doomed by their devotion:

> The round sun swings in thin green skies like to
> a tumbling apricot;
> Through the clear peace there shivers not a sound
> except the sudden cries
> Of men like birds on coral isles, a-singing in the
> bread-fruit trees,
> Of men like fish in opal seas, a-swimming round
> with cruel smiles.
>
> .   .   .   .
>
> We are those Christ has crucified, and sent into
> the bitter ways
> To spill our blood and drown our days in the
> sea's pitiless waste tide.
> And as we drag God's wide blue cup for those
> His souls that perish there,
> In the fierce sun's unflickering stare our own
> souls shrivel and parch up.

II   Three Days

Three Days was published in October, 1919; about half of the twenty-nine poems have to do with the war ("Yesterday"), several others present the post-war world ("Today"), and the rest deal with various matters ("Any Day"). The reviewer in the *Athenaeum* commented: "Miss Macaulay is one of the most interesting of contemporary poets. She always has something to say, something intelligent and original." And he added that "she is a very accomplished metrist" (December 26, 1919, p. 1401). The "Dedicatory Poem," which begins

> The lovely and comic earth, when you go by,
> Waves wide hands full of comic and lovely things,
> Seeking to hold the praise of your flitting eye

depicts a personality halfway between the naïve early-Georgian joyousness of Lucy, in *The Lee Shore,* and the alert intellectual irony of Rome Garden, who will appear in *Told by an Idiot* (1923); presumably the reference is to Naomi Royde Smith, to whom the little book is dedicated. But the poems that compose the book show a world not lovely and only wryly comic.

The war poems include neither "patriotism" nor sentimentality. "The Shadow" tells of a bombing raid: "Bright fingers point all round the sky, they point and grope and cannot find./ (God's hand, you'd think, and he gone blind.) . . . The queer white faces twist and cry." In "Revue," a soldier in London on leave, whose world has been "for too long emptied" of all "but blind desire, and cold and jokes, and frozen mud," is drawn by the lights into a theater in Leicester Square: "And there, bright-lit, was the mad unreason which was the world, the world he knew." He comes out "happy and glorious/ Like the king, or the driver of a bus . . . ." The fog of London and of war closes him in again. In "New Year," peace, if it comes, is but "the derelict babe of strife" and helpless: "War's orphan, she,/ And ungrown mother of wars yet to be . . . ." The idea is sound, but the allegorical concept is inadequate.

Five poems, "On the Land, 1916," bring back the personal, lightly comic approach. "Driving Sheep" tells of this cold predawn chore:

> And old as the world, from out fleece dew-pearled,
>   Gazes each meek sheep-face.
> Dazed with sleep, and numb, the sheep-girls come,
>   And open the field gate wide.
>
> .   .   .   .
>
> Unreasoning, blind, each poor meek mind
>   Takes its thought from the sheep next ahead.
>
> .   .   .   .
>
> And . . . counting the sheep . . . we sway . . . into sleep . . .
>   And trail along . . . foolish as they.
>   [from the slightly improved *Augustan* version]

In "Hoeing the Wheat," backs aching from hours of work under the hot sun,

> We hoe up thistles and dandelions,
>   And all the plantain brood,
> And sometimes by mischance we hoe
>   A swathe of People's Food.

"Spreading Manure" describes labor on the wet clay in a sleet-laden northeast wind; the land-girls cheer themselves with grim humor: "It must lie quite close and trim, till the ground/ Is like bread spread with marmalade." Peace finally comes and brings back the survivors; in "The Adventurers," those who return are "strangers from foreign lands."

Of the poems not about the war, the best is "The Pond," first published five years earlier in *Poetry and Drama* (II [September, 1914], 284).[2] Presenting a rendezvous of passionate lovers, whose relationship is fraught with difficulties, it opens with a description of nature that is extremely appropriate, but surprising in a love-poem:

> Weed-bound, green as grass, the pond lies,
>   With a crazy, hole-riddled tin
> Battered and broken, riding ship-wise
>   On the water's warm green skin
> That bears, like a floor, the weight of June.

The place seems to be one where words will be caught and held for later listeners:

> Oh, lest of our incommunicable
>   Passion and pity, they
> Weave idle dreams and tales to tell
>   Through some slow summer's day
> We'll whisper not: but we will keep
>   Quieter than noon is long.
> We will be still, more still than sleep,
>   Lest our weak words do us wrong.

This poem, the Dedicatory poem, and three of the comic poems of "On the Land" are the only ones that are not somewhat disappointing in comparison with those of *The Two Blind Countries*. Friends say that Rose Macaulay had a haunting lifelong love of poetry; and, indeed, she wrote poems occasionally throughout her life. But her talent profited from a freer medium, where her thoughts could generate their own rhythms and develop unhindered their own curious, questing forms.

CHAPTER 4

Fiction, Essays, and Journalism, 1919-1930

I Introduction

W HAT NOT and *Potterism*, appearing in 1919 and 1920, gave Rose Macaulay a wide reputation for brilliance and, rather unjustly, for "caustic" wit. *Dangerous Ages*, though basically tragic, was overlaid with comedy; *Mystery at Geneva*, a light parody of detective fiction came out next; and *Told by an Idiot* unrolled its forty-four years of history in a comic ambiance. In 1924, before the publication of the very funny *Orphan Island*, an article in *Bookman*, "Some of Our Humorists" (Gerald Gould, LXVII [October, 1924] 1-4), was accompanied by photographs of Max Beerbohm, G. B. Shaw, J. C. Squire, P. G. Wodehouse, E. V. Knox, a few other men, and Rose Macaulay.

Brilliance and causticity were qualities popular among the post-war sophisticates; but, among the more conservative public, any depreciation of sentimentality was apt to be judged unkind. One critic reclared: "Rose Macaulay is one of the wittiest writers going. But she makes me as uncomfortable as a patch of nettles."[1] Some thought her flippant; in a serio-comic "Auto-Obituary" in 1936, she defended herself against this charge: "Those who called her a flippant writer failed to understand the deep earnestness which underlay her sometimes facetious style and the sober piety which she had inherited from her ecclesiastical forebears" (*Listener*, XVI [September 2, 1936], 434). As for causticity, though her wit was on occasion caustic, it was seldom so; and it was aimed at ways of thinking, not at persons. Frank Swinnerton wrote in the early 1930's: "To me, Rose Macaulay has always seemed one of the kindest and least affected of all English literary women. She does, it is true, bring her mind to bear upon the conversation, and she is a little brisk . . . ; but that is all" (*TGLS*, 298). Elizabeth Bowen and Mary Ellen Chase were among others who wrote of her great kindness.[2] If Rose Macaulay found the world full of subjects for raillery, she also found it full of occasions for delight. The lyrical quality of *The Lee Shore* reappears in *Dangerous Ages*, *Told by an Idiot*, *Orphan Island*, and *Crewe Train*.

Each of her works of fiction during this period involves a different scheme and a different relation to "reality." There are two ironic reinterpretations of utopia (*What Not* and *Orphan Island*); parodies of the detective story (*Mystery at Geneva*), the South Sea Island adventure (*Orphan Island*), and the treasure-hunt (*Staying with Relations*); a nearly traditional representational novel (*Dangerous Ages*); a historical tapestry with dramatized episodes (*Told by an Idiot*); a semi-"stunt" novel (*Keeping Up Appearances*); a witty but earnestly crusading political satire (*Potterism*). The tones include gay nonchalance, bitterness, a sympathetic recognition of tragedy, detached derision, and sheer fun. The "implied author" (see ch. II, sec. 1) continues to be a major source of delight, enhancing each mood. These works mix, although in different proportions, the characteristic elements of the "novel" and the "anatomy."

The characters continue to be generated by the needs of the dialectical confrontation. They are ordinarily "created" characters –their actions are based on acutely observed reality, but, like Chaucer's or Dickens' people, they are to some extent projections of certain human tendencies; and their creator is interested in their essence rather than in their moment-to-moment existence. Thus, her presentations combine general judgments and skillful impersonation.

Occasionally in these books a "journalistic" element–an authorial disquisition that gets out of hand and is developed at a length disproportionate to its relevance, or a series of *obiter dicta* on trifling details of the manners of the day–intrudes. Such elements find more effective expression in the two collections of brief essays and in the articles for newspapers and periodicals, where full development is appropriate. These essays grow from a continuous reconsideration of life and almost always involve some skeptical reappraisal.

Rose Macaulay's irony–usually emotionally mild in its criticism, but deadly in the mechanics of its wit–arises from the view that not only the nature of things but also man's own ignorance and stupidity doom most human undertakings, and that the mind is wise to find amusement in observing the incongruities around it. The warmth of her temperament, however, and her urbane graciousness bring tolerance and sympathy to qualify her detachment.

II What Not, a Prophetic Comedy

As the war continued into 1917 and 1918, there were those who were giving more and more thought to the problems of the peace, although in some quarters the subject might be ruled taboo. Rose Macaulay, writing *What Not, a Prophetic Comedy* at this time, speaks of "the days when Peace had not yet arrived and discussion of it was therefore improper, like the discussion of an unborn infant" (21). *What Not*, which was already bound in November, 1918, had to be witheld from publication until the following spring because (according to the prefatory note) "a slight alteration of the text was essential to safeguard it against one of the laws of the realm." This legal hindrance was, as it were, a transposition into real life of the subject-matter of the book: governmental interference.

In this anticipatory satire of the post-war world, the government has established numerous agencies, among them the Ministry of Brains. Its function is "the propagation of intelligence in the next generation" (12). Everyone is classified according to his intelligence; and, in order to spread the available amount of intelligence as far around as possible, those persons in the highest category are rewarded if they produce children by allying themselves in marriage with persons somewhat below them; if both members of the couple are in the medium category, each baby costs them a heavy fine, and so on down. Allowance is made for persons not generally superior but gifted with one great talent; but, with even the highest rating, a person whose family has a strain of mental deficiency is denied certification for marriage. Such a one, in this charade, is, naturally, the Minister himself.

What Not is very slight, a vehicle for various satirical shafts; but its lightly sketched characters comprise a chorus of considerable variety and one star–the dazzling, unforgettable Kitty Grammont. Holding an important post in the Ministry, Kitty, at twenty-eight, "something of the elegant rake, something of the gamin, something of the adventuress, something of the scholar, with innocent amber-brown eyes gazing ingenuously from under long black lashes, a slightly cynical mouth, a small, smooth, rounded, child's face, a travelled manner, and an excellent brain, was adequately, as people go, equipped for the business of living." She was "one of those who see no reason why an intelligent interest in the affairs of the world should be incompatible with a taste for Eve. She enjoyed both classical concerts and new revues. She might be called a learned worldling" (7). Her view of the question of make-up (mooted at the time) is typical: ". . . having been given by heaven such an absurd thing as a human face, what could one do but make it yet more absurd by the superimposed gaieties? You cannot take a face as a serious thing; it is one of nature's jests, and is most suitably dealt with as the clown and the pierrot deal with theirs" (28).

Kitty feels no disapproval of an arrangement that shocks the village of Little Chantreys, where her brother, a young veteran exhausted by the war, has his home: he lives with a delightful, "pagan" revue star and their baby–but marriage it cannot be, for her husband, although not wanting her for himself, will not divorce her. The situation that engendered tragedy in *The Making of a Bigot* gives rise here, four years later, to light comedy; the revue star, with her rich and resonant drawl and amiable ways, is merely another joy to the reader.

Of course, the uncertified Minister and Kitty fall in love; and, after a brief attempt at renunciation–for the extremely unpopular program of the Ministry could hardly survive such a desertion (Kitty herself has always viewed the program as little better than a joke)–they decide in favor of emotion. The Minister insists on marriage (free love is still "a step backwards" in his eyes, although Kitty is willing); they are loyal enough to the cause to marry secretly (181). But during their honeymoon–which they spend swimming at Varazze–they are recognized; and, in a cataclysmic ending, the Ministry falls. The lovers laugh "ruefully" (235).

Throughout the book there is a neat balance between demonstrations of the urgent need for diminishing the stupidity of the population and of the inadequately realistic conception of human beings that mars all authoritarian projects. An effective bit of strategy consists in having part of the satire presented through the consciousness of young Ivy Delmer, who commutes daily from her father's vicarage in Little Chantreys to the Ministry; she is beginning to perceive the mental condition of her family through the Ministry's eyes. Hearing her father preach, even she regrets that such a great force as religion is "in the hands, mainly (like everything else), of incompetents . . . who did not understand it themselves and could not help others to do so" (55). Perhaps the brightest spot in the book is the gathering together in church on Brains Sunday of the village population, including the sophisticates weekending with Kitty's brother. Mr. Delmer's sermon is smartly intercalated with the mental comments of these persons, who, priding themselves on their distance from the vicar, are seen to be at least as far from each other.

The protest against authoritarianism is given a subtle inward turn; Kitty thinks: "There must be in many people some undemocratic instinct of centralisation, of autocratic subversion of the horde of their lesser opinions and impulses to the most dominant and commanding one, a lack of the true democrat's desire to give a chance to them all. They say with the Psalmist, 'My heart is fixed,' and 'I have chosen the way and I will run it to the end,' and this is called, by some, finding one's true self. Perhaps it may be so; it certainly entails the loss of many other selves . . . ." She adds ruefully: ". . . and possibly the dropping of these, or rather their continual denial and gradual atrophy, simplifies life" (169).[3]

III   Potterism

The light "prophetic" charade *What Not* was followed in June, 1920, by a much more complex work—*Potterism, a Tragi-Farcical Tract*, a fictional attack on an actual contemporary form of harmful gigantism, the sensational press. During the war, the press as a whole had undergone such unprecedented development under the leadership of Lord Northcliffe and Mr. Aitken (later Lord Beaverbrook) in conjunction with the political maneuvering of Lloyd George that it had become, in effect, a branch of the government. As a tract, *Potterism* expounds, in its essay elements, the theory that the power of a sensational press is made possible by the attitudes of the encircling public–their refusal or inability to think, their preference for conventionality and emotionalism as against precise thinking and a disciplined search for facts. As a satire, it frequently simplifies the Potters to types and even to figures of farce. As a "novel," it probes deeply into human motives, tracing Potterite attitudes to the general human susceptibility to deep fears and neurotic greediness; it also presents the consciousness of three persons–Anti-Potterites–who are capable of experiencing tragedy.

In "Miss Rose Macaulay's new and coruscating entertainment" (*Spectator*, CXXIV [June 19, 1920] 883), which was so widely acclaimed in Britain and the United States that the author was henceforth a well-known public figure, the press lords are represented by Mr. Potter (later Lord Pinkerton). The Potter twins, Jane and Johnny, have intelligent, disciplined minds; but, swayed by the instinct to "grab" and vitiated by spiritual laziness, they are eventually drawn in by the vortex of the press. Ancillary to this Potter solar system is Mrs. Potter (Lady Pinkerton), its moon, who under the pen name of Leila Yorke, swings the tides of feminine emotionalism by her untiring production of novels. (Several actual women novelists are named whom she resembles.) Claire Potter, the older daughter, has the mindless, hysterical nature that her mother's novels encourage. Although functioning in the structure of the book mainly as types, the Potters are shown frequently enough at close range to add vividness to the work by their individual traits.

In opposition to the Potter way of life, the author has set three persons, all representative of "positions": Juke, a spiritually perceptive young clergyman; Gideon, the "hero" of the opposition–a precise-thinking and sensitive young Jew; and Katherine, a young woman scientist of great delicacy of feeling, who serves almost as the spirit of reason. The plot deals with the gradual subversion of most of the "Anti-Potterites" by the insidious lures of Potterism. Katherine alone remains entirely free. Gideon, fighting to maintain his Anti-Potterite periodical, *Fact*, is, nevertheless, tempted by Jane Potter's cool efficiency; on a visit to Russia, however, he is killed by two opposing mindless mobs.

In an attack on the abuses of journalism, there is an appropriateness in using a form of fiction that itself includes journal-istic elements–passages that are, in effect, essays or short articles. Some of the critics, although praising the book, raised questions about its tone or its form. The reviewer for the *Times Literary Supplement* thought that Rose Macaulay, in her opposition to the over-emotionalism of the Potter press and of "Leila Yorke," was being unnecessarily austere and was denying herself the normal expression of "tenderness." He regretted the absence of those moments in some of her earlier novels when "a gust of deep tragic feeling swept over the scene . . ." (June 3, 1920, 883). To later readers, however, trained in systematic understatement during the decade that was then just beginning, the senseless waste in Gideon's death would seem to make its tragic point well enough.

The same reviewer found "no good reason" for the device of dividing the narration between "R.M.," who "tells" the first and last parts, and Gideon, Leila Yorke, Katherine, and Juke, who "tell" the other four. Undoubtedly, there is some awkwardness in the management of the six parts. The author certainly does not "tell" her own two sections–the style is impersonal and extremely crisp; and the three Anti-Potterite accounts seem intended for no particular reader or audience. Perhaps the formula of "bearing witness" in a trial is intended. But of first importance to this novel is the sense of individual human beings pitting themselves against the juggernaut of Potterism; and the efforts of Gideon, Katherine, and Juke–as well as the pity of their inevitable failure –gain greatly by their individual testimonials. As for Leila Yorke's part, this could not possibly have been presented in any other way with equal effect; and it is one of the wittiest sequences that Rose Macaulay ever wrote.

Despite the notion in some quarters that the "novel of ideas" is a misconceived form, since it must be devoid of drama, *Potterism* is highly dramatic. It contains the usual sources of drama in overall plot and in scene, although directly presented "scenes" do not make up as large a proportion of the book as they do in a typical "illusionist" novel. Primarily, the work is dramatized through the author's ironic style. The brilliance of her irony carries on a combat with the sentimentality and the unimagina-tiveness of the forces she attacks.

The opening paragraph indicates at once the importance of

style in this novel: "Johnny and Jane Potter, being twins, went through Oxford together. Johnny came up from Rugby and Jane from Roedean. Johnny was at Balliol and Jane at Somerville." The wooden simplicity signals the roles of Johnny and Jane as types, and it also prepares for the discovery in them of a certain stolidity, which, despite their intelligence, causes them to fail more and more obviously to meet the imaginative standards of Arthur and Katherine. The paragraph continues: "They were ordinary enough young people: clever without being brilliant, nice-looking without being handsome; active without being athletic, keen without being earnest, popular without being leaders, open-handed without being generous . . . ."

With this relentless series of clichés the author not merely continues her "placing" of these two intelligent but spiritually mediocre young people; she also, by her style, indicates a superior level of cleverness, of which they fall short. The sentence continues, presenting the standard of perceptiveness of the Anti-Potterites: ". . . as revolutionary, as selfish, and as intellectually snobbish as was proper to their years, and inclined to be jealous one of the other . . ." and finishes: ". . . but linked together by common tastes and by a deep and bitter distaste for their father's newspapers, which were many, and for their mother's novels, which were more." The surprise ending carries on the criterion of cleverness, to which is added the preciseness of the final sentences: "These [novels] were, indeed, not fit for perusal at Somerville and Balliol. The danger had been that Somerville and Balliol, till they knew you well, should not know you knew it."

The second paragraph indicates that actualities will be used; there is a journalistic bit of offhand book-reviewing: actual novels are referred to; and there are passing references to contemporary novelists. The book progresses with discussions of relevant topics between characters, with short essays, and with dramatized passages. When World War I breaks out, the author is able to compare reactions by having each of the young people speak for his "position." During the war, conversations between Jane and the author's *raisonneur*, Katherine, bring out the irony of the fact that Jane (and those she stands for), despite her intellectual Anti-Potterism, cannot resist profiting quite Potterishly from the chaotic situation.

The author offers a paragraph on the wartime press, her irony clearly indicated by giveaway expressions and journalistic clichés:

No one could say that the Potter press did not rise to the great opportunity. . . . With energy and wholeheartedness it cheered, comforted, and stimulated the people. It never failed to say how well the Allies were getting on, . . . what indomitable tenacity and cheerful spirits enlivened the trenches. The correspondents it employed wrote home rejoicing. . . In times of darkness and travail one cannot but be glad of such a press as this. So glad were the Government of it that Mr. Potter became, at the end of 1916, Lord Pinkerton, and his press the Pinkerton press.

At the end of the paragraph the perceptiveness and humanity of the Anti-Potterite speaker is adduced, to bring out even more strongly the fakery of the press itself: "With it all, he remained the same alert, bird-like inconspicuous person, with the same unswerving belief in his own methods and his own destinies, a belief which never passed from self-confidence to self-importance. Unless you were so determined a hater of Potterism as to be blindly prejudiced, you could not help liking Lord Pinkerton" (30-31). This close-up leads to the next bit of dramatized action, in which, in the spring of 1919, Jane makes her next abdication from Anti-Potterite principles by accepting the marriage proposal of Hobart, the young editor of her father's most important paper, and so crossing the emotional love felt by her sister, whom the young man had courted at first. These events are presented with every illusionist device: there is no author comment, the physical elements of the scene are made vivid, most of the action is in dialogue, and Clare's misery is expressed in interior monologue.

Part II is presented by Gideon, who is used by the author very economically. This brilliant and sensitive young Jew, whose grandparents had been massacred in a pogrom, is himself a tool against anti-Semitism. His courage in the war and the loss of his foot make him initially sympathetic to even those readers who would tend to be antagonistic to his views. His periodical, *The Weekly Fact*, has as its program to judge each issue "on its own merits, in the light of fact." Gideon observes: "That, of course, was in itself the very essence of anti-Potterism, which was incapable of judging or considering anything whatever, and whose only light was a feeble emotionalism" (55). In view of his editor-ship, it is appropriate for him to comment, in his man's voice instead of the author's, on Labour leaders, Lloyd George, various forms of government, war poetry, and canting speeches. His Russian connection makes it all the more appropriate for him to discuss the mooted Russian situation. Then there is the Peace Treaty, the July, 1919, miners' strike, the condition of the Church of England, and socialism.

Gideon's intellectual discipline, as he serves as the author's mouthpiece on these subjects, is dramatically vivified by his manner: "The trouble about the Labour people was that so far there was no one of constructive ability; they were manifestly unready. They had no one good enough. No party had. It was the old problem, never acuter, of 'Produce the Man.' If Labour was to produce him, I suspected that it would take at least a generation of hard political training and education" (77). Some of Gideon's views are expressed at gatherings related to Jane's marriage to Hobart, and his narrative ends with his awareness of being drawn to Jane–a symbolic development; capability, pragmatism, and physical stolidity offer security in spite of being recognized as spiritually second-rate. Gideon walks Jane home from Katherine's and is standing holding hands with her when Hobart, whose journal had been feuding with Gideon's *Fact*, comes in; he speaks insultingly to Gideon.

Part III is narrated by Lady Pinkerton, under her pen name, Leila Yorke; and the author's satire in this section reaches pure farce. The chief "event" in the novel is presented here: "The Terrible Tragedy on the Stairs." A few minutes after leaving Gideon and her husband together, Jane hears Hobart fall down the stairs and finds him dead. She phones her mother an abridged account–all Leila Yorke needs to set her type of prose gushing forth. Part III is, in fact, a book review in the form of parody. Written in the style of sentimentalists, it presents their self-deception: "Love and truth are the only things that count. I have often thought that they are like two rafts on the stormy sea of life, which otherwise would swamp and drown us struggling human beings. If we follow these two stars patiently, they will guide us at last into port. . . . For Love's sake, then, and for Truth's, I am writing this account of a very sad and very dreadful period in the lives of those close and dear to me" (101).

In her worship of Truth, Leila gives her full faith to a spiritualist; and she hates Gideon for a "spiteful" review of her latest novel, one that he had not written. In her chapter "An Awful Suspicion," after stating her fear of a campaign against her husband's press by Gideon's *Fact*, she suddenly perceives in a flash that Hobart's fall was no accident. A stranger to self-doubt, she makes systematically tragi-farcical misinterpretations of everything she can learn about this Jew; and soon she is confidently spreading her informal charges from circle to circle. She partly convinces her cautious husband of Gideon's culpability, and he sees in a Gideon case a great coup for his press. Only he and his wife must be careful to keep any mention of their daughter Jane out of it.

Part IV is presented by Katherine, a young woman described by Gideon as one "whose brains, by nature and training, grip and hold" (71). Her quiet, precise thought "places" the confused emotionalism of Leila Yorke. This contrast is pointed up in a conversation during the railroad strike of October, 1919, when Leila says:

"Of course, They hate us. They want a Class War."
Jane said, "Who are They, and who are Us?" and she said, "The working classes, of course. They've always hated us. They're Bolshevists at heart. They won't be satisfied until they've robbed us of all we have. They hate us. That is why they are striking. We must crush them this time, or it will be the beginning of the end."
I said, "Oh, I thought they were striking because they wanted the principle of standardisation of rates of wages for men in the same grade to be applied to other grades than drivers and firemen."
Lady Pinkerton was bored. (154-55)

Katherine's discussion of the railway strike constitutes an essay on the thoughtless slinging of jargon that characterized press utterances on this occasion: "The strike was rather like the war. The same old cries began again—carrying on, doing one's bit, seeing it through, fighting to a finish, enemy atrocities (only now they were called sabotage), starving them out, gallant volunteers, the indomitable Britisher, cheeriest always in disaster (what a hideous slander!), innocent women and children." This last phrase she finds particularly idiotic. When a paper on the strikers' side shows a starving striker and his family and asks "Is this man an anarchist?" she comments: "The question . . . was obviously unanswerable without further data, as there was nothing in the picture to show his political convictions. . . ." And she continues: "The Pinkerton press blossomed into silly chit-chat about noblemen working on underground trains. As a matter of fact, most of the volunteer workers were clerks and tradesmen and working men . . ." (152-54). At the end of her narrative, she quietly states that she herself has long cared for Gideon "more than for any one else in the world" (166).

Part V is largely dramatized, for it involves the climax of the melodramatic part of the plot. It is presented by Juke, the young High Church clergyman who, although a nobleman's son, had gone into the war as an enlisted man, not as a chaplain. At a gay party, Juke is revolted when the thoughtless crowd starts bandying about a limerick based on the assumption that Gideon had murdered Hobart. The next morning the Pinkerton press opens its bid for a sensational revelation at the expense of *Fact* with a front page paragraph headed "The Hobart Mystery. Suspicion of Foul Play." At this point the plot's most ironic turn takes place. A miserable, but yet self-dramatizing, girl seeks out Juke; it is Clare, Jane's supplanted sister. She confesses how, after Gideon's departure, she had offered her sympathy to Hobart, but had been rebuffed, whereupon, stung once more with frustration, she had blindly shoved him, causing his fall and death. Juke, commenting meanwhile on the self-deception of such penitents, sends her home to reveal these interesting facts to Leila and the press lord.

Part VI, again, is "told by R. M." Hobart's death is made to yield one more bit of fun at the expense of Leila. From Clare's carefully edited account of what had happened, Leila jumps to the sensational conclusion that Hobart was making "advances" to Clare. Preferring this assumption to the embarrassing facts, Clare makes no attempt to undeceive her and is soon believing this version herself.

Jane gives birth to Hobart's child, assuring the physical continuation of the Potter line, and looks forward to her gradual spiritual seduction of Gideon, to whom she is now engaged. Meanwhile, Gideon discovers that his own periodical has begun to follow Potteristic gods. The author shows him as in an allegory: ". . . a pathetic figure . . . the intolerant precisian, fighting savagely against the tide of loose thinking that he saw surging in upon him, swamping the world and drowning facts" (236). He resigns his editorship; and, becoming something of a Picaresque Saint, he makes a trip to Russia, partly to gather facts and partly to look up any remaining neighbors of his murdered grandparents.

One evening, walking through a London park, Jane sees a Potter press placard: "DIVORCE OF A PEERESS./ MURDER OF BRITISH JOURNALIST IN RUSSIA." Trying to defend a Jewish family, Gideon had been beaten by Whites and then killed by Bolshevists. The author meditates: "A placard for the Potter press. Had he thought of that at the last, and died in the bitterness of that paradox?" The book ends with the ironic amputation of a Biblical passage: "And little Charles Hobart grows in stature, under his grandfather's watching and approving eye. When the time comes, he will carry on."

The journalist-novelist has produced a tightly constructed work. The unity is achieved largely by the use of irony. From the start, the language indicates an exterior view of the Potter clan, a conception of these characters as types; for only occasionally are they viewed so closely as to affect us as individuals. Hobart, who must die, is kept so distant that his death presents no risk to the tone. The three other Anti-Potterite characters are also kept close to their "positions." Two tragic events involving them—Katherine's losing Gideon to Jane, and Gideon's frightful death—are caused by elements of life identified with Potterism and so become subordinate to the main movement of the plot, which demonstrates that Potterism can be successfully opposed only by individuals who, as in a tragedy, pay for their freedom with their lives or with a major renunciation. But, as in comedy, Potterism can ironically discomfit itself through its overweening self-assurance.

The varying of the distancing of the characters, from the distance of satire to the close-up of a "natural" view or of an interior monologue, is facilitated by the linguistic flexibility, which, from the opening page, allows the author to move between ironic farce and controlled awareness of tragedy. This changing is aided also by the use of the voices of four other speakers besides the author.

The discussion of the actualities of the 1914-1920 period, such an important element in the book, is limited to those topics related to the theme, Potterism. Perhaps the greatest temptation to an author in a work of this sort is to stray to tangent topics, or to engage in discussions at a length or with a weight disproportionate to the "novel" elements. This temptation the author has almost entirely avoided.

IV Dangerous Ages

Writing in 1926, Stuart Sherman recalled that *Potterism* had been "dedicated, a bit pedantically, to 'the unsentimental precisians in thought,' " and he commented: "People who hankered to be 'unsentimental precisians' were not so few as one had feared" (85 [see ch. IV, n. 1]). By the next spring, the novel was in its sixth impression. In May, 1921, *Dangerous Ages* came out; although very unlike its predecessor–perhaps partly because of this fact–it too achieved a wide popularity. It is the only one of Rose Macaulay's novels to fall into the category of what are usually considered "women's novels." Men may, of course, read these with profit; Sherman testified: "It is my impression that no dozen novels of my time have given me so much authentic information about womankind as this one."

Dangerous Ages was described in a German dissertation as a retort to Karin Michaëlis' *The Dangerous Age* (1912), a startling Danish novel widely read in its day.[4] The Danish author, whose heroine was in her forty-third year, designated by her title the time of the onset of middle age. But Rose Macaulay observes: ". . . we may say that all ages are dangerous to all people, in this dangerous life we live" (epigraph). Women at four different periods of life are the heroines: Mrs. Hilary, at sixty-three; her daughter Neville, at forty-three; her daughter Nan, at thirty-three; and Neville's daughter Gerda, at twenty. Each is assailed by problems brought about partly by her own temperament, partly by her particular period of life, and partly by the impingement upon her of each of the other women. Only grandmamma, at eighty-four, has achieved a state of peace.

Neville, still fully in possession of her lithe beauty and her fleetness at tennis and swimming, is becoming obsessed with the speeding away of her lifetime; how quickly, in fact, time "was sweeping them all along–the young bodies of Gerda and Kay leaping on the tennis court, the clear, analysing minds of Nan and Rodney and herself musing in the sun . . ." (20). Neville has to fight down her envy of her husband's independent professional life (she had given up her own promising career as a medical student at marriage), her horror at eventually losing her agile strength, and her dread of becoming like her mother. For Mrs. Hilary, who, unlike her children, has never had a capable mind, is a mass of inchoate prejudices, jealousies, and desperate boredom. She has always been jealous of her daughters' and sons' affection for each other; now she is jealous of her sons' wives and of any attentions her children give to grandmamma. She cannot enter family discussions because her mind is directed only toward the personal–it is "stuffed with concrete instances and insusceptible of abstract reason" (29); examples are given of such a mind thinking on topics of the day. For a time she finds solace in pouring out her favorite memories to that father-figure, the psychoanalyst.

Sherman found this novel remarkable for the feeling which the author permitted herself; "she is more or less in love with all these women who are trying to make something out of the little interval that is theirs . . ." (87). Even Mrs. Hilary, stupid and dishonest, is allowed her pathos. But the author's "love" is chiefly accorded to Neville and Nan. Neville appears in the delightful opening scene, getting up at five o'clock in the summer dawn of her forty-third birthday to put on her sand shoes, throw a coat over her pajamas, make herself some tea, spread some bread with marmalade, and slip through the wet garden for a swim in the stream: "She shivered ecstatically as [the wind] blew coldly on to her bare throat and chest, and forgot the restless birthday bitterness of the night–forgot how she had lain and thought, 'Another year gone, and nothing done yet' . . . . Done by her, she of course meant, as all who are familiar with birthdays will know" (1-2). Later in the day she thinks, despairing–"No, it probably didn't matter at all what one did, how much one got into one's life, since there was to be, anyhow, so soon an end" (21).

As for Nan, all of her ages have been difficult. She has always been exasperated with her mother's stupidity, sometimes to the point of violence; at thirty-three, part of her irritation is caused by her recognition in her mother's bad moods of tendencies of her own, and her consequent fear of arriving at the same point. Nan is "an excellent literary critic, a sardonic and brilliant novelist," whose amusement in "investigating the less admirable traits of human beings" is so gratifying that she does not strive against "her worst fault"–a "cynical unkindness" (16). Her unconventionality with intellectual men friends has caused talk; lately she had begun to realize that her friendships have been "stimulants" and that she has no "permanent contacts with life."

Although caring nothing for causes, Nan has gradually fallen in love with a very earnest Quaker, Barry Briscoe, who wants her to marry him; but she hesitates to give up her independence. She has long had a gay, comradely relationship with an unhappily married artist, Stephen Lumley, and she recognizes that they understand each other better than she and Barry do. But "each left the other where they were. Whereas Barry filled Nan, beneath her cynicism, beneath her levity, with something quite new–a queer desire, to put is simply, for goodness, for straight living and generous thinking, even, within reason, for usefulness" (149). (This passage, with its perception of the devotional aspect of love and its acute recognition of the individual's revolt in "within reason" might serve as a microcosm of *Dangerous Ages*.) When her niece Gerda begins to write and publish poems, Nan realizes that she is old enough to be jealous of the oncoming generation –why should they "trespass on her preserves?" (17).

Gerda does indeed trespass. Nan has put Barry off so long that he concludes she cannot love him; and Gerda too thinks so–or if Nan does love him, in this post-war world of England's million excess women, they can "share" him (184). When Gerda, her brother, and Barry join Nan in Cornwall for a bicycle holiday, Nat at last gives Barry an opening for his proposal and finds that he is gazing off at Gerda. Nan's sudden sense of impotent jealousy, her humiliation at having to share the intimacy of a hotel bed with her successful young rival, and the conflict between her adult desire to mother her physically fragile niece and the hatred that tempts her into leading Gerda into a succession of competitive trials-by-athletics are presented with great insight and constitute the most powerful part of the book. Gerda lacks her aunt's skill and is terrified when Nan leads in bicycling down precipitous cliff paths, but she is prevented by youthful honor from sensibly desisting. She follows along blindly and, in effect, wins, by breaking some bones (180).

Nan flees to Rome, where Lumley, suffering from incipient tuberculosis and separated from his wife, wants her to live with him. Miserable over her loss of Barry, she continues to delay making such a decisive commitment. But when her mother, too obtuse to sense any of the agonizing complications of the situation, hastens to Rome to condemn Nan and to insult her supposed paramour, Nan responds by promising Lumley to join him in Capri.

The novel closes with another Hilary sister–who as a social worker is perhaps incongruously given something of the "detached, ironic, cool" nature of Rosamund Ilbert–saying: "Life's so short, you see. Can anything which lasts such a little while be worth making a fuss about?" (269) This dismissal is not, however, the finding of the novel as a whole. As the *Times Literary Supplement* reviewer declared: "If her charm is mainly in the humour and a quaintly conversational manner of writing, perhaps the deeper and more abiding quality of her work is its sense of the tragic struggle with self that rages in every bosom. There are scenes in this book, enacted within a human soul, so terribly poignant that in witnessing them one has almost a sense of personal intrusion." On such occasions, "Miss Macaulay, for all her stern repression of tears, which she reserves for beauty rather than pain, rises to a level which only her own deliberate effort keeps from being undiluted tragedy" (June 2, 1921, 352). The novel was awarded the Femina-Vie Heureuse prize in 1922.

V Mystery at Geneva *and* Told by an Idiot

Having pre-eminently succeeded with two major works in eleven months, Rose Macaulay amused herself with a slight piece, *Mystery at Geneva* (1922), her only detective story; but, as might be expected, it is a comic parody of this genre. What plot it has exists only to afford opportunities for mildly satiric observations on fanatical nationalism, traditions of hatred, and foibles of journalism. A game element is built in: at the end, it is revealed that the hero, a born loser, is really a young woman. Looking back, the reader recalls how phrases and incidents have lent themselves to unobserved admission of this fact.

The next year, 1923, saw the publication of *Told by an Idiot*, which Joseph Wood Krutch described as a "brilliantly executed satire," through whose pages, "liberally sprinkled with exploding bombs of wit," the author leads her three generations of characters (*Nation*, CXVIII [March 12, 1924], 288). The *Times Literary Supplement* reviewer, after acclaiming "the radiant energy that distils through everything she writes," made the point that the novelist has here produced "a sympathetic as well as a brilliant book." This "précis of the social, political, and religious events of the years 1879-1923" is "done with an ease and thoroughness that disguises the solid industry of the feat, the patience and penetration required to assemble just the incongruous, ridiculous matters that illuminate her theme–that history repeats itself mechanically like an idiot, that life is a tale full of sound and fury, signifying nothing" (November 1, 1923, 726).

The opening, which the author said was based on a recurrent event in the life of Matthew Arnold's younger brother, Tom, typifies the struggles of conscience of the period (*L*, 111). One evening in 1879 "Mrs. Garden came briskly into the drawing-room from Mr. Garden's study and said in her crisp, even voice to her six children, 'Well, my dears, I have to tell you something. Poor papa has lost his faith again.'" Through the years this gentle parent had changed from an Anglican clergyman to a Unitarian minister, to a Roman Catholic layman, to "some strange kind of dissenter," to "a plain agnostic, who believed that there lived more faith in honest doubt than in half the creeds," and sometimes back again (1). These phases are reflected in the names of his children: Victoria, "named less for the then regnant queen than for papa's temporary victory over unbelief"; Maurice, "named for Frederick Denison"; Rome, the second daughter, "named less for the city than for the church"; Stanley, the third daughter, "named less for the explorer than for the Dean"; and so on (1-4). The rhythmical changes continue until his death in 1914. The *Times Literary Supplement* reviewer commented: "This pilgrim's progress related with a disarming simplicity is in Miss Macaulay's best vein."

Short chapters–coming in for close-ups of individuals, moving away for the more general view found in quoted bits from contemporary journals, gazing sometimes from a point of aeonic detachment, or probing into someone's secret agonizing–present the lives of the Garden generations through the "Victorian," "Fin-de-Siècle," and "Edwardian" periods and on to the "Georgian" and the time of writing. If the Gardens "matter less than their projector's sayings about them, her gay disquisitions, her enchanting excursions" (*Times*), they are interestingly representational types; and Rome and Victoria's daughter Imogen are among the author's unforgettable characters–the one, a created character; the other, a recollection of the author's childhood.

While the other daughters and sons of the Gardens are recognizable, according to the author, in every generation–the gay, elegant, flightly girl who as wife and mother becomes a leading hostess in her conservative circle; the eager, devoted girl who all her life throws her whole energy into a succession of causes; the placid, practical girl; the young man who spends his life trying to rectify false opinions; and the young man who enjoys exercising his finesse in the business world–Rome represents the spirit of detachment, the ironic eye, the latest form taken in Rose Macaulay's fiction by that aspect of her own personality that was first projected in Rosamund Ilbert. Rome is described at thirty-one:

> She was of middle height, a slight, pale delicate young woman.
> . . . She was a woman of the world, a known diner-out, a good talker, something of a wit, so that her presence was sought by hostesses as that of an amusing bachelor is sought. She had elegance, distinction, brain, a light and cool touch on the topics of her world, a calm, mocking sceptical detachment, a fastidious taste in letters and in persons. She knew her way about, as the phrase goes, and could be relied on to be socially adequate, in spite of a dangerous distaste for fools, and in spite of the "dancing and destructive eye" . . . which she turned on all aspects of the life around her. (65-66)

So Rome proceeds through the remaining decades of her life. But in these later years her awareness includes, unknown to those about her, another dimension, that of tragedy. For a friend, the

writer Frank Jayne, and she had fallen in love; declaring his passion, he had had to tell her that he had unwisely married a
woman in Russia and was a father; although he was separated
permanently from his wife, she would never consent to a divorce.
For some months Rome refuses to consider an alliance with him
because of "her own private standards of decency and taste." But
the rightness of the conflicting claims becomes more and more
uncertain to her. Without the love for which Frank Jayne pleads,
and which Rome wishes to share with him,

> . . . harder and harder and cooler and more cynical she would grow,
> as she walked the world alone, leaving love behind. Was that the
> choice? Did one either do the decent, difficult thing, and wither
> to bitterness in doing it, or take the easy road, the road of joy and
> fulfilment, and be thereby enriched and fulfilled? And what was
> fulfilment, and what enrichment? What, ah, what, was this strange
> tale that life is; what its meaning, what its purpose, what its end?

Having renounced love, one would lie "drowned, dead beneath
bitter seas" (93). Just as Rome comes to a decision, which the
reader is left to divine, Jayne is murdered. The readers four
decades later could recognize in this account the agonizing moral
struggle that Rose Macaulay herself had been enduring. It is one
of the most moving pasages in all her novels.

Nevertheless, donning the armor of the comic spirit, the author
manages to thrust elements of melodrama and even farce into this
sequence of events. Contrasting with Rome's "civilized" self-con-
trol, Jayne's wife is depicted as a Russian revolutionist out of
vaudeville; she comes weeping and raging after him to London,
dragging along her two "little bears" (85). London is full of
plotting Russians, and one of these, a cousin of the wife's, who is
enamored of her, melodramatically–before Rome's eyes–stabs
Jayne in the back. Although not lending itself to artistic integra-
tion, the "Russian Interlude" is entertaining.

Imogen is a character known by the author from within. At
eight, she day-dreams, loves reading poetry, is fascinated by
words. During Nansen's lecture in the Albert Hall "she imagined
him on the *Fram*, sailing along through chunks of floating ice,
and on each chunk a great white bear. Floes, they were, not

chunks . . ." (148). Like her creator, she too "had always meant to be a sailor" (154; *L*, 14). In her imaginings "she had always, ever since she remembered, impersonated some boy or youth as she went about" (177). She hates the abdications required by young-ladyhood. It appears to Imogen that other people are "balanced," that they have "none of the dark and cold forebodings, the hot excitements, the black nightmares, the sharp, sweet ecstacies, the mean and base feelings" that assail herself (236).

All the while, the observations on the world in general proceed at a merry speed. Vicky, in 1880, is displeased that her favored suitor is "not yet in the aesthetic push; he was, instead, in the Foreign Office, and took no interest in the New Beauty. Velveteen coats he disliked, and art fabrics, and lilies, except in gardens, and languor except in offices, and vice except in the places appointed for it" (26). In 1880, when Maurice and Stanley talk of "freedom," Rome comments: "There's one thing about freedom, . . . each generation of people begins by thinking they've got it for the first time in history, and ends by being sure the generation younger than themselves have too much of it. It can't really always have been increasing at the rate people suppose, or there would be more of it by now" (39).

The election that swept the Liberals into power early in 1906 appears in its particularities against the background of the author's feeling of the futility of all party changes. All the members of two generations of the family, of varying political persuasions, go to one of London's central open spaces where the election results are being "proclaimed by magic lanterns on great screens and flung to the sky in coloured rockets." While the adults make triumphant or resigned comments, the young people lay two-penny bets with each other. Imogen ponders the *noli episcopari* hypocrisy of statesmen; if she were elected, she would come right out and say "I sought and wanted office . . . . I simply love being in power . . . and I hope I'll stop in for ages." While Stanley, foreseeing now a quick granting of votes to women, rejoices "Now we'll show the world," and Maurice cynically assures her that "women's suffrage is merely the House joke," Imogen is turning the bursting rockets into cross-riming lines of poetry (222-25; see ch. II, sec. 1, "Two Hymns for St. Andrew's Day").

The device on Rome's shield is "signifying nothing." When

Stanley, home from Oxford, talks of all the jobs we "ought" to do, Rome replies: "The only job worth doing in this curious fantasia of a world, as I see it, is to amuse oneself as well as may be and to get through it with no more trouble than need be. What else is there?" To her sister's exasperated "Why do you think we were born, then?" Rome replies, "Obviously because papa and mamma got married" (40). It is to be observed, however, that whatever Rome does, she does well; and, if she works at no "jobs" and refuses even to write, she works methodically at thinking and is the cause of thought in others.

The author and her characters continually attack cant expressions. On "the sanctity of the home," Rome, who has had a glimpse of Jayne's home, inquires: "Why do people think that sanctity is particularly to be found in homes . . .?" (75; see ch. IV, sec. 7). In the spring and summer of 1900, when those who are disgusted with the Boer War and want a negotiated peace are simply dismissed by the Jingoists as "Pro-Boer," Rome observes: "The Latin word 'pro' has been found always very useful and insulting" (172).

In an article on Rose Macaulay's novels in the *Times Literary Supplement* in 1950, the writer said: "Some of her novels are really animated essays," and he found that some of the passages paralleled in *A Casual Commentary* "appear more at home in the volume of essays than in the novel (May 12, 292). A brief passage here and there–"Keeping House," for example–may be judged irrelevant. (This is developed into one of the best and most relevant passages in *Crewe Train.*) But the book is a fusion of narrative and essay; the persons are for the most part embedded in the background as figures are in a landscape painting or tapestry. In fact, totally impersonal elements–the long lists of events and publications of a particular year that are supplied from time to time to give the chronological bearings–prove exciting. It is rather the detailed presentation of Imogen, delightful as it is–as she plays Sherlock Holmes with her brother, rides the underground on Sunday morning, and climbs trees–that makes a hole, as the French say, in the two-dimensionality of the unrolling scroll.

As for the title, Professor Robert Morss Lovett declared that it "suggests an animus that goes beyond the intention of Miss Ma-

caulay's satire"; and if it were not for certain "flippancies (and
for the fact that the title spits at life) *Told by an Idiot* might be
used as a textbook in modern social history as taught in our colleges" (*New Republic*, XXXVIII [April 16, 1924], 211).

VI   Orphan Island

At the end of *Told by an Idiot* Imogen left for a year's holiday
in the South Pacific, and thirteen months afterwards Rose Macaulay took all her readers there. At the booksellers' in the grey
London November of 1924 *Orphan Island* must have been a
sunny boon–as, indeed, it still is. Cyril Connolly, writing eleven
years later, called it her best novel.[5] It is certainly a work in
which the elements are well controlled. Like *Views and Vagabonds* of 1912, it starts out with a fantastic event–only more so.

Miss Charlotte Smith, an Evangelical country clergyman's
daughter, thirtyish, "set forth in the year 1855 to conduct some
fifty orphans, of various nationalities and all of them under ten
years of age, from East London to San Francisco, where an
orphanage had been provided for them by a wealthy philan-
thropist . . . ." They rounded the Horn and started north, but they
were never to recross the Line; for, in an uncharted area of the
South Pacific, they met with the usual foul weather and sunken
reef. Miss Smith said her Anglican prayers for the mercy of Provi-
dence; Scottish Jean, the nurse, calmly awaited whatever fate
God had "writ in His Book"; the atheist-Catholic Dr. O'Malley
tucked necessaries and a bottle into his pockets; and the captain
superintended the life-boats (5). He, most of the crew, and a few
orphans were, unfortunately, lost; but these other adults, and
forty orphans, managed to reach a coral island.

The next day, however, under Third Mate Thinkwell, the crew
basely made off in the boats. Some months later, Miss Smith was
persuaded by the doctor to put aside her objections to his views
on religion and his experiments with fermented juices and to
marry him, by the Scottish rite. He saw no need to mention a
wife home in Ireland; and Jean, too, held her whist, since nature
will have its own and sin is better committed unknowingly. As a
wife, Miss Smith gradually came to share the doctor's bottle but
not his irreligion; and in one quarrel (ten children had mean-

while been born to them) he threw at her the fact of her adultery. That same day he was eaten by a shark.

From these events, narrated in the pietistic style of that period, the story jumps to the present–1923–when Mr. Thinkwell, a lecturer in sociology at Cambridge, "a very amiable, learned, and gentleman-like man," a widower of fifty-three, with two grown sons and a daughter, learns of his ancestor's act of desertion and receives the rough chart made at the time. He and the young people proceed at once to Tahiti–to the extreme delight of nineteen-year-old Rosamond, whose real life has always consisted in island dreams; charter a small schooner (the *Typee*); and, far off the sailing routes, come upon Orphan Island.

Physically the reef, lagoon, shore, flora, and fauna realize all the descriptions in all of Rosamond's island books put together. Hanging face downward from a rock, "she saw the small sea world where scarlet and yellow and green crabs, some bearing their shells on their backs, some on their stomachs, scuttled about among tiny, bright-coloured fishes, and pink and yellow and blue trifles which were, William said, copepods. Tiny anemones opened and shut like flowers; little sea worms wriggled among waving hydroids; translucent shrimps, egg-laden, passed beamily about their business" (138). On a forest path they find that "a thousand sweetnesses, like fleeting thoughts, assailed the hot, still, brooding air. In the dense green overhead monkeys chatted brightly, and radiant parrots uttered sharp, staccato cries, while paradise and humming birds flashed brilliant colours on the woody gloom. With soft, continuous thuds cocoa-nuts fell on the emerald grass . . ." (59-60). Some details appear to have been seized upon rather nonchalantly–for example, the breadfruit that Rosamond finds so delicious when eaten raw.

As in any island book worthy of its ink, the shipwrecked manage to fashion from native materials and with the very few tools they have with them all the necessities of a comfortable, civilized life. Dr. O'Malley in his ten years on the island had proved himself an ingenious man. Rosamond is delighted to find the charming bark and palm-leaf houses, the clothes of pounded bark and feathers, the objects made of shells, the delicious foods and drinks. Here, she thinks, she can lead a life unhampered by the tiresome demands made by social conventions and by the exigencies of the weather, both so annoying in England.

But life on the island is not the idyll that Rosamond supposes; in fact, its complications turn out to be of the greatest interest to her father's sociological study. Miss Smith—every head bows when her name is mentioned—is still living, ninety-eight years old, up the hill at Balmoral, and still rules. The island has a parliament on the narrow base she had known in mid-century England; and her dutiful son, Albert Edward Smith, is Prime Minister. All the land "belongs" to the Smiths, while the Orphan class are the laborers. In fact, it is difficult for the Smith descendants to avoid idleness because "none of the work except being in parliament . . . is Smith" (233).

The Thinkwells also learn that the Sabbath is strictly kept and that all through the years Miss Smith has ordained the clergymen and for their Sunday sermons given out the Bible text—from memory, for unfortunately no Bible had been saved from the wreck. Miss Smith is not at a loss in finding divine sanction for her wish that none of the islanders depart on the Thinkwells' schooner: "And the Lord said unto Adam, Be thou content with the garden which I have given thee, and see thou run not after every new thing" (159). She has caused moral poems and proverbs to be carved on many of the trees, so that the people, as they go about, are automatically admonished. In the segregated schools (Smith and Orphan), natural history is presented anthropocentrically. Miss Smith keeps watch and ward on manners and morals.

Writing in 1927, John Inglisham said: " 'Orphan Island,' one of her best if less popular books—as innocuous as it is delightful, was received by some critics with exclamations of indignation, surprise or pain, as being a particularly unkind satire on Victorianism" ("Rose Macaulay," *Bookman*, LXXII [May, 1927], 107). It is difficult to see how the book could be considered "unkind." As for "Victorianism," such critics failed to take account of many explicit statements referring to the contemporary period, of parallel satire in others of her books directed toward her own times, and of the cultural lag in much of society in the early 1920's (see Braybrooke's attack on *Crewe Train*). Those of the islanders whom she satirizes represent less a bygone age than the non-thinking, the cliché-ridden, the humorless, the sentimental, and the dispensers of humbug, who are timeless.

Thus, "teachers of the new type" are imparting to their pupils "via plants, birds, and animals" the sentiment that human gestation and birth are "very holy. Very beautiful. A very wonderful arrangement of God's" (214)–a typical approach to the subject in popular periodicals and more advanced elementary schools in 1923. This approach disgusts Mr. Thinkwell: "Why not let them know at once . . . that it is one of the very worst, silliest, most inefficient, and most infernally inconvenient and dangerous arrangements in all nature?" (215). The passage of time had worked changes among the island people in about the same proportion as at home: minorities had launched an esthetic movement–the young men wearing flowers over their ears–and more than one egalitarian political rebellion. As in *Told by an Idiot,* the author is pointing out that, even under different circumstances, these human developments keep appearing.

Although one aspect of the book contrasts the dream of a free, open earthly paradise with man's jealous and finicking obstruction of its enjoyment by his fellow men and even by himself, the author never loses sight of man's ineluctably ridiculous plight on this planet: those who sleep outdoors in the lovely island night are kept awake by "stars, centipedes, land crabs, birds, monkeys, and other ingredients of the woodland scene"; and Charles Thinkwell, throwing himself down by a "sedgy lake" to moan his rejection by that minx Flora Smith, finds, like Hardy's Bathsheba, that "the marshy smell of stagnant water was in his nostrils" and that the golden stars "were caught in green, weedy scum, floating there with sleeping water-birds and a thousand crawling insects" (294-95).

The irrational desire of many–not all, for some fear to lose caste in a new locale, or do not want to bother–of the islanders to get away, to go to their dream country, Great Britain, meets with the fate it deserves through the final superb act of that remarkable woman Miss Smith. While the islanders are compulsorily celebrating her Birthday in church, she secretly allows the convicts a sail as a Birthday Treat and so makes sure of the irreversible departure of the schooner. Old Jean, baffled at the very moment when she hoped to fulfill her lifelong desire to get back to Aberdeen, now renounces her loyalty and reveals the truth of Miss Smith's "marriage" and the consequent bastardy of all the Smiths; enraged, Miss Smith has a stroke and dies. In the year that follows, political and economic changes remarkably like those in England in the twentieth century rapidly take place, under the direction of the new Prime Minister, Mr. Thinkwell. Who can say, though, whether "the deterioration almost inevitable in politicians" may not before long set in (318)?[6]

Orphan Island is expertly narrated. The traditional expectations of desert-island stories are made part of the game. The story-line is broken into by no journalistic essays. The large proportion of dialogue serves to indicate not only the personality of each character but also the period—from 1855 to 1923—on which his customary thinking is based. Sunny good humor informs all the satire; there is no indignation but only absurd fun, a joyous recognition of incongruities, and endless witty observations.

On the island there is a class of Negro laborers, whom "no one pays"—"they don't expect it" (65); they are all named Zachary Macaulay, after the Abolitionist. From the shipwreck, Miss Smith had managed to save Bunyan's *Holy War* and Emily Bronte's *Wuthering Heights.* The Thinkwells learn that a housewife named True-Heart Jenkins has just killed her husband with a jam made of poisoned berries; when they meet the rebellious son of the Prime Minister, they find that he is called Mr. Heathcliff Smith. Dr. O'Malley had saved a Latin book—he was given to quoting in that language with the self-satisfaction of Chaucer's Chantecler —but no one can read it. Miss Smith has long since dismissed the doctor from history; when she, rather boozily, tells Mr. Thinkwell "Ten children we had," he senses that the pronoun is the royal "we" (92).

Rosamond is perhaps the most delightful of the series of varying but similar non-intellectual young girls who appear in many of the novels. At home she enjoyed food and playing with her puppy, but hated dressing up and callers and being indoors. She knows a great deal about the one subject that interests her—South Sea islands; she has lived in dreams of them. She has "greatly loved"—schoolmates, "Sir Ernest Shackleton, that Mr. Mallory who climbed up Everest, . . . the Rajah in the *Green Goddess,* Joan of Arc, . . . several athletes and naval men, seen from far . . ." (151).

Any love in return seems to her a sacrilegious thought. She is one aspect of the girlhood of her crisp, erudite creator.

VII   A Casual Commentary, Catchwords and Claptrap, *and Journalism*

In 1925 Rose Macaulay published *A Casual Commentary,* a collection of thirty-nine short essays. Some of these twit and gibe at the assumptions of the unthinking public and the daily press; some view with resignation the frailties of the human race; some hint at the author's enthusiasms or gently urge certain human decencies. The reviewer for the *Nation and Athenaeum,* contrasting the tempo of her style with that of the leisurely traditional essayists, pointed out that "Miss Macaulay is frankly a journalist, and her articles keep time with the tramp of daily city-goers. She can be read in the tube and even enjoyed there." He mentions her "brisk, Aristotelian sentences" and finds that "she has retained her fastidious precision of thought . . ." (XXXVIII [December 5, 1925], 380). The *Times Literary Supplement* reviewer, finding a sameness of tone, observed that they make "very good reading" when read one or two at a time. There is a considerable variation, however, in the amount of pertness with which the topics are treated; and, in general, the essays farther along in the book uncover a fuller sympathy with the divagations of mankind. As this reviewer said, ". . . she is not superior, in the unkind sense" (December 10, 1925, 855).

In attacking set ways of thought, she frequently uses the strategy of assumed naïveté. Since we "choose" and "select" in so many trivial matters, these terms and the acts they refer to would seem all the more appropriate to a matter of much more importance, hence—"How to choose a religion. How comparatively seldom this problem seems to be discussed" (5). And, after a few examples of the glib advice that our journals give us on other choices, although not on this one, she continues: "There are many ways of selecting a religion." Moving imperceptibly from this innocent beginning to an attack on blind bigotry, she manages to turn the "faith of our fathers" ideal into something quite different: "Some people scarcely select, but merely retain that, if anything, which was imparted to them in youth. For such indiscriminating and conservative souls the problem does not arise."

After suggesting some techniques of choosing that would require a lifetime, she assists by offering a catalog of the sects that pokes—or sometimes jabs—each at its feeblest point. Her comments move quickly backwards and forwards between unexceptionable generalities and startling particularities: "Jews have had a poor time for a good many centuries. They used to be kept in ghettos, and to have their teeth extracted by bad dentists until they gave up their money to the government, and even now they are disliked by many people, such as Mr. Hilaire Belloc" (13). Tricky devices of style bring sudden brilliance: "Some people are Theosophists, and have many successive lives; others are Mormons and have many simultaneous wives; other are Pagans suckled in a creed outworn." Back of the fun, however, is her lifelong haunting sense of spiritual experience: ". . . the only really dull thing is to have no religion at all. If you really cannot manage any, you had better instead keep pet dogs, children, or a motor-car. But your life will, whatever you keep, be a shallow affair, lacking background. It is better to have a religion" (13).

A series of ten essays considers the choice of a career. Recalling nineteenth-century tracts, she exclaims: "How carefully ought young men and women to consider this weighty question!" There follows what the *Times* reviewer called a "demurely mischievous" discussion: "Women have one great advantage over men. It is commonly thought that if they marry they have done enough, and need career no further. If a man marries, on the other hand, public opinion is all against him if he takes this view" (17). In "Problems of a Journalist's Life," she explains the job of the reporter: "You may, in fact, report anything you like, provided that you report it in the right spirit, with the correct amount of élan, gusto, and amaze" (26; see ch. IV, sec. 9). "Problems of the Citizen" is among a few of the essays that are perhaps over-pert. In "Problems of a Writer's Life" she observes: "Any form of work is insufferably tedious, and this not least (though assuredly not most either)." Once written, the manuscript "may go forth from the writer to return with a faithfulness passing the faithfulness of the boomerang or the homing pigeon" (46-47).

The essay "Problems of the Social Life" guys the problems in an American book of etiquette and declares that "the root problem . . . is How to Escape" (66; see ch. IV, sec. 8). One problem she carefully dissects is that frequent one of the hostess who wishes to have absent from her table the dull spouse of a bright married friend. The *Times* reviewer observed: "To play well, in this manner, with externals, . . . the smartness must spring out of hard, critical sense. And Miss Macaulay's generally does." He finds "a good deal of the eighteenth-century poise about her," and speaks of "her eighteenth-century sense of fitness . . . ."

The inquiry "Into the Sanctity of the Home," a devastating attack on this canted subject, develops at much greater length Rome Garden's comments in *Told by an Idiot*. If this sanctity is destroyed by divorce, then clearly it "has no reference to the lofty qualities of those who dwell" in the home "but is a mere *ipso facto* attribute attached to a life led by a married couple. A restricted definition . . . ." She continues: "What homes have sanctity? Is a bachelor or spinster home insusceptible of this grace . . . ? Can a flat have sanctity? . . . a boarding house? . . . a hotel? . . . And is sanctity a gift undivided and complete (like Orders) . . . or is it more like a sense of humour, which has degrees?" The use of the plural form is puzzling: "Could a home lose sanctity and yet keep some sanctities?" (96-97).

And so these essays continue, taking aim at the current linguistic idiocy of equating the word "suggestive" with "indecent" (101-3), at the limited understanding of certain groups who insist that all people should be brought to think alike in religion, at the fatuousness of the statement "The only real crime is not to live life to the full" (in an outrageously funny essay) (173), and at the ridiculous simplification of history that underestimates the jollity, cleverness, and degree of education of pre-twentieth-century women.

Not all is satire: ". . . we are a haunted race, fleeing from silence and great spaces, feeling safe only when surrounded by warm, comprehensible, chattering humanity like ourselves" (115). People, she finds, "are mostly likeable" (125). And she pleads for religious tolerance: "For most of us there is no such thing as the true religion. There are only the varieties of religious experience, as manifested by each person" (124). In "even a little" belief in God there is "wonder" and "beauty" (185).

Catchwords and Claptrap was published the following year

(1926), in the second series of the Hogarth Essays, edited by Rose Macaulay's friends Virginia and Leonard Woolf. It continues the inquiry "Into Human Speech" in *A Casual Commentary*. In the opening paragraph the writer gives a description of "language": "this fantastical currency, minted by the requirements of human thought and feeling, circulated by the urgent desire we have to convey these somehow to our fellows, so precisely, so delicately wrought and cast into exact and minute forms, so skilfully adapted to the commerce which is its purpose, and, having been so shaped, shaping in its turn thought itself, stamping it ever freshly with intricate designs . . ." (5). Although tolerant of the rebellion of "the free spirit of man" against established usages, she finds sloppy use of words and phrases an unfortunate debasement of this "currency" (6-7). And she inquires into the psychological reasons back of certain classes of misuse.

During the 1920's, as through the rest of her life, Rose Macaulay was continually being asked to write articles, and not only by literary journals but by the popular press. With other persons of note, she made her contribution to such series as "If I Had My Life to Live Again" (*Daily Mail*, August 25, 1928), "My Best Day's Holiday" (*Daily News*, June 20, 1924), "What Most Interests You—and Why?" (*Daily Herald*, August 13, 1928), and "Have We Done with Hell Fire?" (*Evening Standard*, March 25, 1929).[7] Her comments are never "flippant"—a term unjustly applied by some critics to her writing—but perceptive and thoughtful. When she is "witty," the wit is a flash of clear sense cutting through the wrapping of humbug. In the second series mentioned, she tacitly attacks sabbatarianism by describing the fun the Macaulay children had every Sunday in Varazze; in the third, she dismisses a list of conventional interests and speaks of language, geography, "abroad," ancient civilizations, and "animal life all over the globe, . . . tropical life and vegetation, . . . the Roman Empire, and Greece, . . . and the study of different religions, and almost any history when wars are not occurring, and any elegant, witty, or otherwise pleasing writings." In the fourth series, she wonders "what qualities in humanity started and kept going this rather excessive conception of punishment?" One of her best articles of the period is "Defamation" in the *Saturday Review*: ". . . is there no such thing recognized by law as dramatic utterance? Is the author responsible for all the views expressed by characters in his novels? . . . You could not make a teetotaller speak against a Martini . . . ." Should the novelist always have someone contradict such statements? Or insert a parenthesis after such comments? (CXLV [June 30, 1928], 830-31).

VIII   Crewe Train

Crewe Train–

Oh Mr. Porter, whatever shall I do?
I want to go to Birmingham, but they've sent me on to Crewe!

–came out in 1926 to take its place with the four earlier brilliant fiction pieces of the 1920's. Less searching psychologically than *Dangerous Ages* and without the purpose of *Potterism,* the erudite frame of *Told by an Idiot,* or the elaborate scheme of reference of *Orphan Island,* it probably exceeds any of them, page by page, in coruscation. It is dedicated to "THE PHILISTINES, THE BARBARIANS, THE UNSOCIABLE" and, in tiny print, "to those who do not care to take any trouble." The opening sentence is a marvel of complex wit: "A Mr. Dobie, a clergyman, wearying of his job, relinquished it, ostensibly on the grounds that he did not care to bury dissenters or to baptize illegitimate infants, but in reality because he was tired of being so busy, so sociable, and so conversational, of attending parish meetings, sitting on committees, calling on parishioners, and asking them how they did–an inquiry the answer to which he was wholly indifferent." The opening words recall at once the dreariness of Wordsworth's notorious "A Mr. Wilkinson, a clergyman." Then comes the jolting view of Holy Orders implied in the word "job." Then the carefully reasoned antithesis that constitutes his proffered explanation–and its devastating presentation of the Church's doctrinal and moral inefficacy. Then his real reason, which further devastates the Church's activities and sets the theme of the proliferation of social activities, which dominates the novel. And, finally, the meaninglessness of most conversation. Three other matters are immediately striking: the sense of a rational civilization given by the architectonic control of this complex sentence and the efficient diction; a glimpse of the irony that is to pervade the book, seen not only in "job" but in the euphemism "relinquished"; and the element of farce in the implied adequacy of Mr. Dobie's proffered twin reasons.

The next paragraph introduces the opposite theme: "Having relinquished these activities, and having just enough money left him by his lately dead wife to exist penuriously without industry, Mr. Dobie looked round for an agreeable and peaceful spot in which to reside" (1). When Mallorca provides inadequate privacy, he takes his "grave, square-faced, brown-legged" little daughter Denham to Andorra; but here again the social aspect of life begins its invasion: "Snared by passion and a desire for household comfort," he makes a second marriage; and soon his Andorran wife has given him a large set of new relatives and four children (5-7). He and Denham perfect their techniques for avoiding conversation, visitors, and (on Denham's part) housework, which she sees as a useless activity. A new interference sets in when Denham is twenty-one, for her mother's relatives—the intellectual, chattering Greshams of Chelsea—make a visit to Andorra. Mr. Dobie unfairly deserts the scene by having a stroke and dying; the relatives then kindly take Denham away with them to London. Rose Macaulay's divertissement has been set up.

In London, Denham finds that civilization implies a mania for proliferation. Among the civilized, literature proliferates: ". . . Uncle Peter [a publisher] poured forth books all the time, as pleased as a cat having kittens, and half the people who came about the Greshams' house seemed to have a hand in writing them. They urge Denham to read many of these. Conversation proliferates: "At one end of the table was Peter, pouring out story after story . . . . At the other end was Evelyn, talking without pause . . ." (59). Down the sides were Guy, Audrey, and Arnold Chapel, being fluent and amusing—and Catherine, whose husband "was to speak in the House that night. It was obvious that any husband of Catherine's would have to speak in the House fairly often" (55). Things proliferate. Denham must not wear in London the simple, comfortable clothes that she likes; for multiplicity of functions has generated a multiplicity of costumes: "trouble indeed, to others and to oneself, seemed to be one of the greatest objects of this strange human life" (50).

Soon after Denham's arrival, the Greshams give a party to which all sorts of clever and surprising people come. The presentation of their party is a complex of acute observation–straight and satirical; fantastic projections are intermingled with authorial reminders of social decencies. Catherine enjoys the party but finds that her mother has included too many people who "did not count. . . . In her view, people ought either to count, or to stay in their own homes." Evelyn Gresham, like her daughter, "distinguished between counting and not counting; and indeed to do this is one of the first social lessons"; the author adds that "one of the next is to be kind to those who do not count" and Evelyn was kind. Guy, who is in the Foreign Office, tells good stories in four languages "and in none of them needed the assistance of fact" (74-76). Humphrey observes that his enterprising mother is pleased with herself for having thought of inviting some visiting lamas before anyone else did; later in the evening his own special guests arrive–a crowd of Sudanese from a Soho dancing cabaret. The party ends at two-thirty in the morning, but each of the Greshams must stay awake for some time talking with one of the others. Denham alone is fast asleep.

During one weekend at the Greshams' country home, to which many voluble, clever guests have, of course, been invited, one of the cleverest, Arnold Chapel, seeks out silent Denham, "the big brown girl in her red jersey," who is shaping a boat with "her strong, practised hands," and declares his love for her (89). They both feel a strong physical attraction. During their engagement, they go to Cornwall with his parents; they fish, swim, sail, and explore the rocky coast; and Denham finds it perfect: "if life with Arnold were to be like this, marriage would be a happy lot" (120). This state is the "Birmingham" where she wants to get off life's speeding train.

Their idyllic honeymoon in Mallorca should be continued, Denham thinks, in permanent residence there; but London life is to Arnold a necessary stimulant. He explains: "One's right at the heart of things there. One's more alive than in other places. One sharpens one's mind on other people's. . . . It's galvanic" (128). She tries to like it. When they are invited out every evening of each week, she finds that the straightforward utterances she ventures on the subjects she knows about–maps, dog diseases, and shore fun–only serve to elicit from her dinner partners clever rejoinders. After useless attempts, she falls into silence, although her aunt has warned her how hostesses feel about "dead spots." The author recounts such an occasion, when the sturdy, handsome girl caught Arnold's eyes on her "in a fond and fleeting look, a swift caress. Yet she knew that she was letting Arnold down, by not talking. In the glance of her hostess, a little later, she perceived no caress" (135).

A new development gives Denham an excuse for refusing some of their invitations and insisting that Arnold go without her: she becomes pregnant. In a book published the following year, *Some Goddesses of the Pen,* the author, Patrick Braybrooke, a Fellow of the Royal Society of Literature, attacked Rose Macaulay for her "extreme frankness" in her sentence "Denham felt, and often was, sick in the mornings" (158). In this sentence about Denham at the time when, as Braybrooke put it, "she is undergoing the trying process of preparing to have a baby," Rose Macaulay's "realism is tinged with an obvious pandering to the disgusting license that certain women novelists take such a pernicious delight in exhibiting" (London, 1927, 45). The existence of such criticism in 1927 proves a cultural lag, even in high places, that critics of *Orphan Island* seemed unaware of. Denham's morning-sickness is important to the plot; for–depressed by it, bored with the physical idleness that the doctor advises, and having no desire for such a stupid encumbrance as a baby–she resumes her outdoor activities and has a miscarriage. Thereupon, Arnold and Denham have their first serious quarrel, which leaves them uncomfortably aware of the distance between their preferred ways of life.

This distance exists, of course, within Arnold himself, who loves to idle about in a boat with Denham but soon becomes impatient again for the intellectual creativity of the analytic life–the life that delights in dividing and subdividing and in designating each detail in terms of the appropriate nomenclature, that continually calls for choices and for judging other people's choices, that offers the game of intellectual thrust-and-parry. Rose Macaulay, herself both Arnold and Denham, loved all her life to swim, to walk in the country, to get away; she tried to simplify her daily life, to escape time-wasting intrusions(*L, passim*); she was a great collector of one of the few types of published material that Denham liked–maps; and as the *Times Literary Supplement* reviewer observed, she could "give an unsophisticated and almost childlike twist to her mind" (October 28, 1926, 742). Nevertheless, she was always ready for social gatherings. In *Crewe Train* she declares: "Talking is one of the creative arts, for by it you build up things that have, until talked about, no existence, such as scandals, secrets, quarrels, literary and artistic standards, all kinds of points of view about persons and things. Let us talk, we say, meaning, let us see what we can create, or in what way we can transmute the facts that are into facts that are not yet" (84).

After the miscarriage, Denham and Arnold spend a month in Cornwall; and this period, with the weeks when Denham remains there after Arnold's return to talkative London, makes one of the most memorable parts of the book. In an old fishing boat Denham "spent absorbed and solitary hours paddling in and out of creeks, landing in sandy, fishy caverns, dropping the plummet deep into green water and hauling it up, noting on the chart measurements, hidden rocks, inlets and caves" (163). One day she finds a secret smugglers' passage that leads to a cave–"fairly dry, and, as caves go, spacious" (165). The upper exit is bricked up under the floor of a deserted cottage on the cliff. In an ecstasy Denham gets Arnold to rent it, and they move in; only to Arnold does she reveal the secret passage. But their life in the cottage and cave, eating fish, gulls' eggs, and unleavened bread–"Less work is my object. Less work, and more time for other things" (207)–soon bores Arnold. And the Greshams immediately want to complicate the cottage with quaint Cornish furniture and pottery.

One day, under the floor, Denham overhears Aunt Evelyn discussing her at length with Arnold. Disgusted with Mrs. Gresham's persistent public analysis of private lives, and feeling that Arnold has broken their marital trust, Denham insists on remaining behind in Cornwall when Arnold returns to London; but she promises–during the night before he leaves–to come soon. Back in the chattering London atmosphere, Arnold cannot keep a secret; he lets slip to Evelyn the fact of the cave, and the day Denham returns to try London again a newspaper article in gushing prose describes her hideout and her "romantic tastes" (217). While Evelyn intrudes on Denham by phone and door to apologize–and to admonish her niece not to go about London in that old sweater and skirt–the unhappy girl thinks of her cliff and cave, the "quiet, misty October sea . . . . Fish waiting to be caught, crabs scuttling round in the rock pools, gulls and plovers swooping and crying between cliff and sea" (222). She goes back out there on her motor-bike–to find the cottage overrun with inquisitive people. Arnold receives word that his wife will bike around the coast for a while.

At this point the author brings the chatterers' creating of "facts that are not yet" to a fantastic development. Evelyn had always hoped that Arnold would marry her daughter Audrey, with whom he works and whose intelligent, gay companionship he enjoys. Her compulsive imagination spins out a story in which Denham, having left Arnold, has become the mistress of a fisherman; and in which Arnold and Audrey come to a passionate understanding. Writing is believing; and, fully convinced, she puts the typescript where Arnold must read it. Although, at his insistence, she burns it, she tells all London about Denham's "fisherman"; worse, her formulation has awakened enough self-consciousness in Arnold to make him feel uneasy and guilty in his friendship with Audrey.

In a scene of foggy December mist dripping from the Cornish gorse and turf, dark and silent except for gulls and foghorns, Noel–the Gresham's young Oxford daughter, quiet and impersonal, walks along the cliff to Denham's cottage and finds her alone with her maps and dog. Arnold, Noel tells her, is ready to move out of central London into relatively rural Buckinghamshire. Denham, too, is ready to return; she is pregnant again, but not by a fisherman.

At the end, in their compromise home–one not so rural but that neighbors are kindly preparing to call–Denham lies obediently on a sofa while her mother-in-law instructs her in how to make work so that the maids will be kept busy each day of the week: "No day without something cleaned. And one room thoroughly turned out each day, too–that's most important. . . . The things all taken out of the room and put back again, you know." And the older woman continues briskly, terminating the book:

". . . it's a great help to have some kind of scheme mapped out for the day . . . . One should begin it right after breakfast–9.30-9.45: see the servants; 9.45-10: do the flowers; 10-11: read the papers and write one's letters; 11-1: serious reading; . . . 4-5: tea and see friends. . . . And so on, do you see? It regularises the day so, and prevents one drifting and idling the time away, as one's often inclined to do. . . . There needn't really be *any* empty moments in one's day, if it's properly schemed out. Think of that! Not one empty, idle, useless minute."

Denham thought of it. . . . (305-7).

Crewe Train's popularity is well deserved, for its debate is central to modern life. Tempted toward increasing intellectuality, toward dealing with ideas of life rather than with living, the skeptic looks nostalgically at Denham's world and its values and asks, Is the unexamined life less worth living than the overexamined life? But he is hurried along nonetheless. Since 1926, only in a few details—vogues for simpler dress, simplification of home furnishings and housekeeping, simpler vacationing—has he been able effectively to rebel.

If Denham is balanced precariously where sturdiness, straightforwardness, and simple appreciations verge on a subhuman way of life, the Greshams' way of life verges on a condition where bad money drives out good, where intellectuality degenerates into triviality and irresponsibility. The conflict between Denham and the Greshams is conceived in terms of recognizable realism heightened with well-controlled comic exaggeration and presented by a witty and economical "implied author"—as in the final four-word sentence.

IX Keeping Up Appearances

Keeping Up Appearances (1928), published in the United States as *Daisy and Daphne*, was described by Cyril Connolly in his review as "a very witty and stimulating book, based on a good idea and winged with a fleet of smaller ones, well constructed and admirably readable" (*New Statesman*, XXX [March 31, 1928], 796). But he and other reviewers pointed out that in some respects it was disappointing.

The "good idea" is a stunt, which is amusing and which offers enjoyment of its technique upon a second reading. It consists in the presentation of one young woman as two through the first two-fifths of the book. Daphne Daisy Simpson, thirty, is the illegitimate daughter of a gentleman, long deceased, and of a farm girl (since, the wife of lower-middle-class Mr. Arthur)–"the jolly, vulgar mother at East Sheen," as the *Times Literary Supplement* reviewer called her (March 29, 1928, 241). Daisy's natural diffidence causes her to conceal her birth. She makes her living by writing columns and novels for the wide public under the chatty, journalistic personality of "Marjorie Wynne."

Educated at a good school, and living for some years with her father's sister, a good writer, Daisy exists also in the allotropic form of the dashing and properly parented Daphne, aged "twenty-five," a jolly companion, and one never at a loss. Although the superiorities are by no means all with Daphne–Daisy is warm-hearted and imaginative–most of those that count with the Folyot family are; and Daisy fights a comical, and of course losing, battle to keep these intellectual gentlefolk, and especially their son Raymond, to whom she–or rather Daphne–has become engaged, from discovering the whole truth. That Daisy's deceptions have served her badly–that Raymond might in the long run have preferred Daisy to Daphne–is suggested. There are some passages of delicate perceptiveness as in Daisy's elder-sister relationship to the Folyots' nervous, keen twelve-year-old daughter Cary–one of the author's most delightful children.

In 1896 H. G. Wells had deplored the degradation of journalism and fiction that had resulted from the great increase in the reading public after the Education Act of 1870: "It is scarcely too much to say that every writer of our time who can be called popular owes three-quarters of his or her fame to the girls who have been taught in Board schools."[8] Rose Macaulay had frequently gibed at books and journalism of this type. Daisy Simpson is a writer who knows better but finds is easier to make her living by writing the chatty woman's-page columns in which concocted general questions on generalized women and "flappers" are "discussed," and by producing novels only a cut or so higher. Daisy's half-brother, a reporter, supplies his paper with the inaccurate, fakely sensational news stories that his editor demands. Aiming her instruction, apparently, at much this same public, Rose Macaulay analyzes numerous passages from such writings, making clear what stupidities are involved. These "essays" on journalistic error are accompanied by others on slatternly linguistic usages, and too often the tone approaches that of carping; attack on language plays too large a part in the treatment of class differences. The triumphant depiction of Mrs. Arthur is an exception.

In the book as a whole, too many unrelated follies are attacked, and not always on sound grounds. Despite its faults, however, it offers many delights. There are such observations by the "implied author" as "To work was nauseating. Daisy would have liked to be as Erinna, who had left a considerable reputation as a poet, but only a few lines of poetry, or Eriphanis, who has left one line, only that is not a very good one. Achievement without labour; that was the ideal. Whereas the common lot of life was labour without achievement" (7). And passages that twit the outdated conventionality of the press: Daisy's brother envisions a heading that would read "Adam and Eve True. Amazing Belief of Bishop" (82). And there is the final incident, when, on shipboard—on the way to lecture in the United States—a bewildered little spirit trying to realize itself, not quite as Daisy, nor as Daphne, is forced by the approach of an admiring woman reader to become, once again, "Marjorie Wynne."

X Staying with Relations

During two months of the winter of 1929-30 Rose Macaulay made her only visit to America. She and her sister Margaret, an Anglican Deaconess, crossed the United States by train and drove down the West Coast with their surviving brother (now resident in Canada) to the Mexican border. Margaret was not permitted to enter Mexico because her religious uniform put her under suspicion of being a Catholic nun; consequently, Rose's excursion into Baja California was disappointingly brief. *Staying with Relations* (1930) makes use of this trip; but two-thirds of it takes place in Guatemala—a country she had not visited. The sources of some of her details are made clear in *Pleasure of Ruins* (1953).

The main idea in the novel—that even a bright young woman novelist may badly misread character—is worked out, as the *Spectator* reviewer observed, "quite arbitrarily and quite mechanically."[9] There is an enlivening series of comic incidents—a treasure-hunt, a kidnapping, and a chase (with a sleek scoundrel in view).

But not all is comic, for the agony of the girl Isie, kidnapped by Indians, and then stumbling lost and torn through the jungle, is presented seriously and well. The final third of the book follows the author's hurried trip through the strangely beautiful country of Baja California.

If the book is, in several of its aspects, disappointingly facile, it nevertheless includes many passages worthy of the author's talent. As for the jungle, it is given here a power and mystery of a sort that would have been inappropriate to *Orphan Island*; and its enveloped ruins, with their proof of human transiency, are the first instance of this symbol that was to be important in her later writing.

CHAPTER 5

Studies, Fiction, Essays, and Journalism, 1931-1940

I Some Religious Elements in English Literature

IN her book on Milton (1934), Rose Macaulay mentioned "that subconscious desire to be employed on some work not creative which often attacks authors undecided as to their next invention, and often unripe for it . . ." (97). Perhaps she was voicing one reason for her having turned, after two somewhat perfunctory works of fiction, to *Some Religious Elements in English Literature* (1931), a little book of literary study for the Hogarth Lectures on Literature Series, published by her friends Leonard and Virginia Woolf. Coming as she did of parents descended from long lines of clergymen–some Presbyterian, many more Anglican–she had from childhood known "days and psalms and creeds and even most of the major heresies!" (*L, 36*). Besides their relatives, the family had always had many friends among the clergy, and they frequently engaged in discussions of various aspects of Church doctrine.

From 1909, when at the news of her brother's death in India, Rose had offered herself as a missionary, until after World War I she was drawn to attend High Church services and, on occasion, retreats (*L, 211*). It was during the period 1914-16 that she had a formal acquaintance with Father Johnson (ch. I, sec. 5), a member of the Cowley Fathers, which was to be revived by a letter from him in 1950 and to flower into the remarkable correspondence between them during the remaining eight years of her life. He recalled seeing her, during one retreat, in "the little, dull, square garden . . . pacing up and down very gravely and slowly, I think *on the grass*, for a long while, *in steadily drizzling rain*, tall and grave and thoughtful, wearing some sort of dark tweed

suit–no overcoat or rain-coat. This she did for a long time"
(*L*, 18).

Several attractive young clergymen and religious laymen appear
in her novels during that period, along with some clergymen who
are at fault for narrowness. A great deal of space in *Non-Combatants* (1916) is devoted to comparing beliefs and church services. After World War I she presented two more delightful clergymen–Jukes and Dr. Garden; but, having entered upon a personal
relationship that the Church would not have countenanced, Rose
Macaulay felt obliged to let her own communion lapse. Among
the matters that she freely satirized during the post-war years
were narrowness of dogma and crude, unworthy services.

Her pursuit of scholarship, evidenced in *Told by an Idiot,* had
been continuing and was to be the mainspring of her writing in
the 1930's. In 1935 she wrote in *Spectator*: "I have already over
a thousand and a half volumes lining the walls of my flat–few
of them written during the last hundred years" (CLIV [April 12,
1935], 605).[1] Now, at the beginning of the 1930's, she wrote *Some
Religious Elements in English Literature* to examine her theory
that "most religious literature was the outcome of some kind of
clash or conflict, and bore stamped on it the nature of this conflict, and the fusion, victory, or defeat which had been its outcome" (5). For reasons of space, this little survey will not be
discussed here.[2] The ideas in the section of greatest interest,
"Anglican and Puritan," were expanded into her historical novel,
They Were Defeated.

II They Were Defeated

Several of the poets in the section "Anglican and Puritan"–
actually Anglican, Puritan, and Roman Catholic–were to reappear
the following year in a book that represents the flowering of
Rose Macaulay's lifelong interest in the seventeenth century:
They Were Defeated (1932), her only historical novel, and the
novel (she recalled in 1951) that she most enjoyed writing (*L*,
59). As an undergraduate at Somerville College, Oxford, she had
majored in history; to quote from her account in a letter to Father
Johnson: "I took the whole of English history (one has to) beginning with the Anglo-Saxon Charters, Villeinage, Sheriff's Courts,

etc., etc. (these bored me rather) but my Special Period, and my Foreign Period, was the 17th century. We had to do Political Science and Polit. Economy, too. I was much interested in most of it . . ." (*L*, 94-95).

The story of *They Were Defeated* takes place during the eight months from October, 1640, to May, 1641, from just before the convening of the Long Parliament until the day of Strafford's execution. The Puritan success in branding as treason Strafford's attempts to harmonize royal prerogative and popular consent climaxed the long struggle between extremist Roman Catholics and Puritans and the intermediate Anglicans of varying views. The desperate politics of the period are discussed by the characters, often hotly, and are seen directing the trends of their thoughts and emotions; but the main purpose of the novel is to present the literary and philosophical life of the time. Specifically, the author takes her readers to Devon, where she revivifies Robert Herrick and the villagers and gentry of Dean Prior, and to Cambridge, where the poets, scholars, clergy, and townsmen of the period come to life.

Sharing the foreground with Herrick are his neighbor Dr. Conybeare and the doctor's fifteen-year-old daughter Julian. Dr. Conybeare is an appropriate though imaginary son of one of Rose Macaulay's Elizabethan ancestors of that name, a schoolmaster; and he is drawn after one of her cousins, a contemporary member of the same family (*L*, 35). In Julian one aspect of the author herself is set back in that earlier period—the scholarly young girl, eager for more knowledge, for a chance to be a writer, for permission to discuss subjects of importance with men as an equal. Herrick's great desire is to have his poetry recognized; while the doctor, a noble-hearted skeptic, tries to win people away from stupidity and superstition. When the novel was published in the United States, the author relates, "the American publishers didn't like the word 'defeated' . . . so called it *The Shadow Flies.*" But, she goes on, "*They Were Defeated* is what it is about. Every one is defeated—Julian Conybeare, Herrick, the Royalists, the Church, etc." (*L*, 27).

The book is the longest of Rose Macaulay's fictional writings, and properly so; for it is a work of thorough scholarship. Out of her knowledge grows one of its great charms–the language. The author states:

> I have done my best to make no person in this novel use in conversation any words, phrases, or idioms that were not demonstrably used at the time in which they lived; though I am aware, for all the constant and stalwart aid of the Oxford Dictionary, and the wealth of literature, letters and journals of the period that we possess for our guidance, that any such attempt must be extremely inadequate; or, at least, that mine is so. I must apologise both for its inadequacies, and to those (if any) who may think that I have used too many words which now sound somewhat peculiar in our ears; ghosts of words. . . . If they should vex any reader, I should be sorry, but would assure him that I have rejected so many more of these ghosts than I have admitted, that I am surprised . . . at my own moderation. As it is, they are not so frequent after all, and can, like other revenants, be ignored. (Prefatory note)

The management of the diction is so skillful that all seems natural. The customary slight formality of Rose Macaulay's style is just perceptibly increased so that the voice of the "implied author" furnishes a background a little nearer to the language of the seventeenth century–a background, in fact, that accommodates itself to increased or reduced distance. Thoughts and indirect discourse assume a style close to that of the period. Finally, direct discourse is, as the author has said, approximately authentic. A passage near the beginning, during one of Herrick's services, illustrates this technique: mischievous adolescents had added a little pig to the harvest decorations in the church, and it has just been removed:

> The last squeals dying away as the disappointed little creature was borne out of the churchyard and across to the parsonage, the congregation settled down, their joke at an end. Indeed, they speedily looked sober enough, for it was Brief Sunday, and their vicar proceeded, since the thread of his discourse was now irrevocably broken, to command them to give their bountiful and liberal contributions to the redeeming of captives in Algiers, taken prisoner by the Moors. . . . Sir John Suckling, just behind [Julian], caught a glimpse of the diamond tears glistening on the lashes of the pale, pretty child, and approved her mightily. A pretty little

maid; an extraordinary pretty, tender little maid, thought he.
Robin must make her known to him, and also the long, copper-
headed wench next her, who looked a gay young spark with a
good spirit. . . . Sir John whispered a question to Mrs. Elizabeth
as they knelt for the prayers. "Why, the Yardes, to be sure," she
replied, in her round, comfortable voice that scorned concealment.
"From the Court, ye know. And t'other little wench is the doctor's" (17-18).

The plot is loosely constructed to permit the illustration—at the
phenomenal level—of certain aspects of the life of the times; but
each incident is symbolic of the contending forces in that fatal
year. Dr. Conybeare is known to be skeptical to the point of
atheism. When poor senile Mother Prowse (the subject of one of
Herrick's lampoons) is hunted as a witch, he tries to make the
villagers see that she is merely mad; unsuccessful, he tries to
defend her in court; unsuccessful again, he gives her poisoned
medicine. His deed is suspected, but wise moderation on the part
of certain of the country gentry prevails over more punitive
counsels. The doctor decides to take Julian to visit her brother
Kit at Cambridge, where both father and daughter can profit from
the intellectual atmosphere. Herrick, who has been tutoring Julian, goes along for a vacation and to try the luck of his poetry
among the poets of the younger generation.

In Cambridge, Julian lives in an excited dream as she sees, in
church and at college masques, the learned and gifted men gathered there. A better scholar than Kit—or than the devoted Giles
Yarde, who finds study a mere bore—she is smitten by the unfair-
ness of the system that bars her. When the poet Cowley hears
that she writes verses, he assumes they are "posies for rings." The
closest she can come to the intellectual life is to attend a small
class for ladies, held once a week by Henry More, the Platonist.

In time, Kit's tutor, John Cleveland, the handsome poet, Latin-
ist, and rhetorician, comes to govern her imagination. Foreseeing
a charming adventure, Cleveland, with Cavalier suavity, finds
occasion to teach the child to respond to his elegant wit and to
his caresses; he perfects his subjugation by throwing into the fire
a thesis she had written for More and by forbidding her to discuss
with him learned topics or matters of state. Let a young maid, he

says, "refrain from seeking more learning than is apt to her sex, for no man asks that of her." Julian protests: "But if she loves books for themselves? Why should she have ever at mind what men ask of her? Mayn't women please themselves ever, then?" (286).

The doctor's older son, Francis, has become a Puritan. Kit, tempted by the romanticism he sees in the prohibited Roman Church, runs away to court to join his new co-religionists. Herrick has been recalled to Devon. While the doctor goes to search for Kit, Julian is left behind to live her dream of love. Even in her passion she grieves that her lover dismisses so much of herself—her inquiring mind—from his affection. At the doctor's return after some weeks of absence, Cleveland must tell Julian that he "frees" her (346). Meanwhile, rioting is breaking out everywhere; and Strafford, the pillar of the Royalists, is arrested. The doctor appoints Francis, who has come from London, to stay with Julian while he goes back to give aid to the endangered Kit; and Francis, unlike his parent, hears the local gossip. Since undergraduate days he has been envious of his elegant, popular fellow-collegian; and, when Cleveland comes to the Conybeares' rooms, it is from an impure righteousness that Francis attacks him. Julian, attempting to stay her brother's arm, is thrown violently aside; her temple strikes a corner of the table, and she is dead. It is the day of Strafford's execution.

Symbolism plays an important role in this novel. Strafford, although making errors, had worked to hold the kingdom together both by supporting the Crown and by urging it toward reason. Frequent references to him serve as fever-thermometers for the State's disease. Dr. Conybeare, writing his compendious attack on human unreason, loses one son to each of the extreme parties; and of his young daughter, who had played the Lady in a performance of *Comus,* her High Church Royalist lover says to her brother the Puritan, "W'have slain her between us" (364).

Dr. C. V. Wedgwood, the historian of Charles' reign, in her Introduction to the 1960 edition,[3] has pointed out the symbolic relation between the seasons of the year and the themes that are presented:

First there are the ripe harvest colours of Devonshire; autumn advances as the witch hunt darkens the story. When Robert Herrick, with his friend Dr. Conybeare and his daughter Julian reach Cambridge it is the time of long evenings, candlelight and blazing fires; the winter is shut out as they talk of poetry and philosophy, just as the menacing political situation, with Parliament threatening the King, is temporarily forgotten. Julian's love story reaches its climax in the spring, and her death on May 12th, 1641 coincides with the execution of Strafford, the minister on whose ability alone the royal cause had rested. The young girl's life unfolds from the autumn when she is still a child at her books, to the spring when she falls in love and dies, with no summer to follow, but only the thunderstorms of the Civil War to scatter and destroy its promise. (15)

The book is packed with memorable scenes: the harvest service in the Dean Prior church, rich with Herrick's thoughts of the various members of his congregation (taken from the record of his own epigrams), his utterances, descriptive details of the permanent and the festival decorations, and Suckling's amorous thoughts; the warm autumn countryside, through which Julian strolls with Giles and Meg Yarde; home life in Herrick's cozy parsonage, with his sister-in-law Elizabeth, his maid Prue, his dog, kitten, and sparrow; Herrick drinking with various friends; the view of Cambridge as Julian looks out from the inn window in the misty pre-dawn; the crowded college masques, with the young men shouting and singing; Cleveland's poetry-reading evening party; the townsmen rioting in a college church; Julian riding in the spring air with frustrated young Giles; and Cleveland holding the dead girl and realizing the tragedy of her brief life.

Then there are the discussions, like the one between various members of the gentry at dinner with the Yardes at Dean Court, in which the author strives to give each side a just representation. Dr. Wedgwood notes that as a child, under the influence of her great kinsman's historical writing, Rose Macaulay had considered Hampden, the sturdy opponent to Charles' levy of the ship-money tax, "her ideal hero. Later in life her views grew wider, and though she was never sure that she liked their politics, she preferred the minds, and the company, of the Cavaliers. Her sympathies were for the clerics and poets and scholars whose harmless lives were disrupted by the Civil War" (13). There are no lovable Puritans in the book. Francis is seen as not recognizing the role played by envy in determining his choice of party; the rioting townsmen who destroy the church carvings and altar rails are moved as much by anger at being excluded from a place of worship which was once open to them as by doctrine; the professional witch-finder is a sadist. He is joined, of course, if less bestially, by most of the gentry, of whatever persuasion.

Managed with expert artistry is the inclusion of bits of poems written by several of the characters–Herrick, Suckling, Cowley, Crashaw, Henry More, Cleveland–and passages that they all know, such as lines from Milton's *Comus*, lines by Ben Jonson, or beloved Latin passages. These fall naturally into place; to these poets the world of the Classics and of their own imaginings gave another dimension to the events of every day, to their love adventures, and to the sudden descent of death. Cleveland's seduction of Julian is attended by passages from poems, including his own witty "Antiplatonick."

After reading *They Were Defeated*, Ralph Strauss wrote in the *Sunday Times*: "I place Miss Rose Macaulay among the three most interesting and distinctive women novelists in England today." He described the work as "an historical novel . . . of a kind that does not often see the light. For it is no costume romance . . . . I know of no other work of fiction which gives such a well-balanced and intimate picture of those curious days or conveys more admirably to us the real excitement of the times. Here, indeed, *is* that England of long ago. . . . It is a fascinating picture which, I cannot help thinking, will give you a truer idea of the times than many of the histories seem able to provide (October 16, 1923, 7). L. A. G. Strong declared: "Her great achievement . . . is not so much that she has lightly blended with her romantic story a deal of learning as that she has succeeded in presenting historical characters without any distortion and has yet made them integral and proportionate parts of the whole. . . . this is perhaps the rarest achievement of the historical writer." He concluded: "*They Were Defeated* is a great book, with a charm which makes affection predominate over respect, and which will ensure that it is taken down often from the shelves, and read, and read again" (*Spectator*, CXLIX [October 22, 1932], 558).[4]

III   Milton

The spate of recreating the seventeenth century produced another work, the little book on Milton, published early in 1934 in Duckworth's series "Great Lives." In the limited space of about thirty-five thousand words, Rose Macaulay attempts to present Milton the man, as the title of the series indicates, rather than the poet—Milton's ideals; his conception of his powers; his relations with his friends, family, associates, and enemies. Professor Alexander Witherspoon, reviewing the book, observed that the author had used "freely and wisely, and after fresh examination of them, the familiar documents and sources as well as the latest studies" of important scholars. In a book of this type, he noted, the reader expects "no important new material"; but he found here some "fresh and at times unconventional interpretations of Milton's life and work." After praising the book for lucidity and artistry, Witherspoon noted that "Miss Macaulay's method is that of a woman, of a wise, tolerant, civilized woman" (*Saturday Review of Literature*, XI [April 27, 1935], 646).

Professor Basil de Selincourt, however, found it less "tolerant": "Her biography of him is in the Strachey style, a little work of art, in its way, but inspired by the dangerous conscientiousness of disillusionment; it is witty, learned, sonorous, devastating; but perhaps not quite detached." In fact, although he agreed that Milton's marriage failed because of his theory of the husband's "arbitrary authority" and because he was "a dull male and a dull master," he found that "on this topic Miss Macaulay is strangely unmerciful," as if Milton were in this respect "so far from good, that his very sufferings might not be pitied. It is almost as if something hypnotic or maenad were mingled with her ruthlessness, so persistent is it . . ." (*Observer*, [January 28, 1934], 5). At this point De Selincourt was perhaps taking his turn at being "devastating"; for Rose Macaulay appears to have tried rather hard to be just to this famous husband. Reminding the reader that nothing is known of the seven years of marriage after Mary's return, she is ready, nevertheless, to pity the marital disappointment of the idealistic, inexperienced husband: "He may have settled down to a life lived on a level which youth had never anticipated, in a mixture of apathy, pity, desire, and cautious hope." In regard to his bitter expressions about spiritual incongruity in marriage, "how much had the anger of a hurt and humiliated man to do with those high words?" (85). This passage is hardly in a "maenad" tone.

Then suddenly the discussion takes a different turn:

> The interesting question remains, what would Milton have made of a clever and cultivated wife? How would he have fadged [got along] with a Dorothy Osborne, a Lucy Hutchinson, an Anne Finch? . . . We shall never know how he would have got on with a wife of these gifts, or how she might have affected his views of her sex. Would Eve, had her creator's connubial circumstances been thus different, have been another type of woman, perhaps even have been permitted to sit with Adam and the archangel at table and join in their cosmic conversation, instead of merely supplying the fruit and nuts and then wandering away to do some gardening, knowing that Adam would tell her afterwards all she needed to know, and doubtless more, of the table talk?

The teasing seems fair enough, for "Milton had educated women among his friends"–he was not without other models when he drew Eve (86). As for the intelligence of his daughters, the author points out the lack of conclusive evidence.

The reviewer for the *New Statesman and Nation* wrote that the book "presents a Milton who could never imaginably have been called gay, cheerful, amiable, or good company" (VII [February 3, 1934], 162). But Rose Macaulay finds this matter enigmatic. For example, during his Italian sojourn, when his "personal charm" is attested by his social success, he seems nevertheless to have been accustomed to speaking on matters of religion with a freedom that embarrassed some of his hosts; for the smoothness of his social relations she gives a great deal of credit to the traditional tolerant courtesy of the educated Italians and to their sophisticated cynicism (50). In dealing with his pamphleteering, she makes clear the political rudeness of the times and the various provocations that he was meeting. She also shows his increasing disillusionment with his own party and his courage in chiding them.

There is some justice, however, in the charge made by the reviewer for the *New Statesman* that the book "makes no attempt to cope with the fact that he was a great man." A similar charge is implied in De Selincourt's discussion; De Selincourt declared that Milton "knew" his "unique stature," whereas Milton's concept of his inborn greatness draws from Rose Macaulay the term "subjective" (140). She does not deny his greatness, but she insists upon its limitations: "His tremendous imagination penetrates chaos and the spheres, but never the human soul, creates for us a universe, a glorious garden, or the very desolation of human despair, but not the subtler play of mind and heart." She sums up: "As a man he was, despite his disconcerting contradictions, of a fundamental simplicity. He possessed an undue share of sensitive, irritable and vaunting egotism . . ." His view of himself as "God's nursling, as his country's prophet, and at the last as a vanquished Titan" and one "always in the right" he must have "politely subdued in intercourse with friends, for his company was esteemed and found agreeable. . . . he died a vanquished and embittered idealist, in a world with which he had never come to terms, nor could" (140-41).

The *Times Literary Supplement* reviewer, after praising the book for "lively writing" and for a background of "up-to-date knowledge of the latest Miltonic studies," remarked on her treating "Milton the youth with much understanding" and also on her realizing "how far in advance of opinion to this day is his matrimonial philosophy." He pointed out her interest in all Milton's feminine dependents. Commenting on "what there is of literary criticism" in her book, he said: ". . . in particular Miss Macaulay makes a good point over 'Paradise Lost': Milton is not only Satan, as many have said, but also Adam, Michael, the Almighty,—all the characters, in fact, except Eve, and she was as he wished a wife to be; such was the egoism of the 'exotic, monstrous mind which shaped' the poem." And he concluded: "To sum up, a most readable account of Milton the man, both well informed and eloquently written" (January 11, 1934, 29).

IV   The Minor Pleasures of Life *and* Personal Pleasures

In October of the same year, 1934–her novel *Going Abroad* had been published in July–Rose Macaulay brought out a compilation of short passages in prose and verse from English and foreign literatures entitled *The Minor Pleasures of Life,* a companion to *The Major Pleasures* by another author.[5]*The Minor Pleasures* was the first of her "pleasures" series; the word was repeated in the title *Personal Pleasures* the following year, and once again in 1953 in *Pleasure of Ruins*. After her death a number of tributes written by her friends were collected in *Encounter* by Harold Nicolson under the title "The Pleasures of Knowing Rose Macaulay."[6]

The Minor Pleasures runs to more than seven hundred pages. The passages are not the usual anthology pieces; some, in fact, had never been published before. The *Spectator* reviewer commended the collection for its "variety . . . a variety which proceeds from a mischievous errant wit" (Dilys Powell, CLIII [December, 7, 1934], 892). He pointed out the particularity of her examples: the compiler "has caught the passion for curious detail characteristic of" the seventeeenth "and the preceding century." As he noted, "part of the fun is in the tabulation"; under "MALICE," for example, are found "Baiting Gibbon," "Libelling Poets," "Ridiculing Poets," "Poor Fielding," "Annoying Envious Men," "Charmed with Scandal," "Hating One's Colleagues," and "Scoring Off Magicians."

Personal Pleasures, a collection of seventy-one short essays by Rose Macaulay, appeared in the autumn of 1935. This collection is very different from *A Casual Commentary* and *Catchwords and Claptrap,* for here are no problems–social, ethical, or personal; instead, each essay is a brief witty disquisition on some pleasure that the author enjoys or has enjoyed. The scheme of wit involves presenting the pleasures in alphabetical order, as in the preceding volume; in neither book is this requirement too exigent–some of the more difficult letters appear to have initiated no pleasure. A program also is involved: each analysis, the author says, will end with the identification of this pleasure's "pain"; the enjoyment of the pleasure, therefore, involves irony.

The several retrospective essays on her childhood are written simply. But the others are in a markedly mannered style that reflects both her seventeenth-century interests and a certain "aunt"-like temper, which, according to Frank Swinnerton, was frequently her mood at that period (*TGLS*, 299), and which can be seen developing in *Keeping Up Appearances* and *Staying with Relations*. The program of wit calls also for frequent allusions and quotations–chiefly from seventeenth-century writers; and for the playing of a game with the reader that involves polysyllabic constructs–both extant and invented ad hoc–from Greek or Latin elements.

Rose Macaulay can do this type of thing superbly, but the staccato rhythm and donnish tone become wearing if more than two or three pieces are read at a time. In "Finishing a Book" she looks distastefully at her product and says: ". . . never more will I write one; nay, I have done, you get no more of me" (199). In "Book Auctions" she introduces bibliophiles, bibliolaters, bibliomaniacs, and, necessarily, the bibliopole (83). The etymological fun tends occasionally to become too self-regarding, and the mannerisms perhaps frequently so. The great number of words with the prefix *en-* seem not to justify their presence: "we lay enwrapt in post-prandial dominical peace" (281), "when your groaning writing-table is so deep ensnowed" (238), "Diana enstagging Actaeon for this ill-judged bagniospection" (350). Many of the recherché Latinisms are, in effect, intrusions: "My newspaper makes me realise, in the improbable event of my ever forgetting it, on to what an exciting, what a tumultuous world, the sun and I matutinally rise" (317).

Rose Macaulay's erudition is a source of delight, but it is sometimes, as in a number of these essays, misused. Four years earlier she had written an essay in *Spectator*, "Autumn Meditations," of which she said, in a foreword: "I have used, in the main, words that were in common use among our forefathers, but are now less so . . . . I will let this essay stand as a counter-blast to modernity, modernism, or whatever the newer fashions in literature may be called. I admit that I am a reactionary. I have no great love for modern English usage, and think our speech had a better ring three centuries since" (CXLVII [November 21, 1931], 700). The essay itself is written in seventeenth-century speech. Her intense interest in etymology exposed her writing to the peril of mandarinism—of using a style directed toward the very few. Fortunately this peril receded after *Personal Pleasures;* for, as the threat of World War II developed, she needed to use her writing for public ends, and henceforth she kept it closely related to the life of the world she lived in.

The descriptions of the pleasures, adorned with amusing far-fetched comparisons–congruous and incongruous–are a middle-aged version of the introductory lines to *Three Days*: "The . . . earth . . . / Waves wide hands full of comic and lovely things" (ch. III, sec. 2). The speaker is grateful for comfort, is pressed for time, tends to choose contemplation rather than action, and never long forgets the irony implicit in any human ease.

There is the pleasure of "Believing," and also of "Disbelieving": "but sometimes a thought troubles me, and I ask myself, should I, many centuries back, have been numbered with those who denied the Antipodes, and the rotundity of earth?" (158). In "Church-Going–Anglican," the service is full of joys, but there are pains too: "These violent Hebrews: they break in strangely, with hot Eastern declamation and gesture, into our tranquil Anglican service, our so ordered and so decent Common Prayer" (122). For an Englishman, "Abroad" is a "delicious . . . prospect," but "is it worth the trouble of . . . ever climbing up the climbing wave?" This avid traveler soon answers that, but on the train platform at Calais new pains arise; she cries to the porter: "But see, there lacks one bagage [*sic*]; where can it be? Oh, Oh, you have left it on the platform over there. Vite, vite, facteur! The train departs. You have not been vite enough; the train is departed. I shall not see my bag again" (17-20).

Parties are a pleasure, and also turning back at the door and seeking solitude instead on the Embankment. Flying and driving are fun, and watching fire engines (partly an etymological pleasure); she shares the excitement that those pyromachs are surely feeling, for all their calm exterior; and she gives way to her innate pyrolatry. The last essay in the book is on "Writing," which

has always been to me, if a rather shame-making, yet an insidious amusement. Wherein lies its charm? Mainly I believe, in arranging words in patterns, as if they were bricks, or flowers, or lumps of paint. That is, to me. Heaven never, I think, destined me for a story-teller, and stories are the form of literary activity which give me the least pleasure. . . . To play with these mixed coins, to arrange them in juxtaposition, to entertain oneself with curious tropes, with meiosis, litotes, hyperbole, pleonasms, pedanticisms, to measure the words fitly to the thought, to be by turns bombastic, magniloquent, terse, flamboyant, minishing, to use Latinisms, Gallicisms, Hellenisms, Saxonisms, every ism in turn, to scatter our native riches like a spendthrift tossing gold–this is the pleasure of writing.

But Rose Macaulay realizes that what the public desires is not these experiments but books, and "how incompetent do I feel adequately to produce these!" (377-81). With these words, the collection closes. The nine books she was yet to write vindicate the superior wisdom of the public's demand.

V   Going Abroad *and* I Would Be Private

In 1933 Rose Macaulay visited the Spanish Basque country, and one result was her most compactly gay novel, *Going Abroad* (1934). Gathered at the Spanish Basque coastal resort of Zarauz are an unlikely group, brought together to satisfy their author's ulterior purposes. After her topics of the early 1930's, it is not surprising to find among them a bishop–in this case, however, the missionary bishop of Xanadu. Mrs. Aubrey, his wife, is a former Cambridge classical don, who for the fifteen years of her rather late marriage has directed her scholarship toward identifying and reconstructing the Garden of Eden.

With the Aubreys is her brother, a fastidious retired diplomat and Dante scholar, Sir Arthur Denzil. Then there is the liberal, elegant, detached Mrs. Buckley; the correct military man, Colonel Buckley; the Buckleys' esthetic and authoritarian son Giles, a student at Oxford; and their honest-hearted daughter Hero (whose great beauty is an atavistic inheritance from her illicit ancestor, Lord Byron). The visitors at Zarauz also include a cosmopolitan couple, M. and Mme Josef, who try to conceal their Basque birth, but constantly proclaim their profession–they are beauticians, with shops in several of the world's capitals. Then, erupting into the town, fresh from a successful "house-party" in Hendaye, come a "crowd" of several energetic young British persons who have "found Christ"; they are Oxford Groupers–members of Dr. Frank Buchman's Moral Re-Armament movement.

In her dedication Rose Macaulay describes her novel as one of "unredeemed levity."[7] There appears to have been some fear among her friends that dull readers would resent her presentation of the Oxford Groupers. The Moral Re-Armament movement, as much as the Basque country, generated the novel. In a letter to her sister late in 1932, she enclosed a clipping about the public confessions at one of the Oxford Group meetings to "show you how right I am not to approve of them." And she continued: "Shall I write a novel about it, after attending some meetings? . . . I should treat it very respectfully, though with some regret. My hero or heroine, seeking religion, would try it, but retire after a time, debauched by and the worse for the experience. But I should need to know plenty about it first, and, in learning about it, I might get converted and stay to pray, you never know" (S, 60).

Though certainly not "converted," she did in a sense "stay to pray"; in the novel–although she teases the Groupers and includes them in the general ironic treatment, indicates their esthetic shortcomings, and brings out the unreasoned aspect of some of their taboos–she continually keeps in the forefront the idea of the danger of quashing any zeal toward good; and she assigns the most unkind utterances about them to an unpleasant, immature character (compare a similar treatment, ch. II, sec. 4). Furthermore, the line of plot projected in the letter did not develop. The heroine is not "debauched by and worse for the experience," but considerably helped by those aspects of it that she–by nature, a skeptic–accepts. Rose Macaulay remained interested in the topic and, shortly before her death, mentioned that she was thinking of reading a certain book on the movement; in this connection she said, "I suppose I should choose 'Love one another' as the essential Christian approach" (S, 231).

That the novel is founded on an important moral debate, as well as an esthetic one, gives its comedy body. Most of the attitudes and incidents in the book are related to the concept of custodianship. The bishop, who meant to use his vacation for rest and study, must face–or (to use a Buchmanite locution that Rose Macaulay deplores) "face up to"–the question of the degree of involvement that he should accept in relation to the young religionists; for they wish him to chair their open meeting at the hotel. His wife and her brother, as pure scholars and liberal gentlefolk, claim the right of detachment. The Buckleys are uncertain as to the extent to which they should attempt to guide their beautiful but confused and unhappy daughter. The Groupers, of course, have been assigned the custodianship of all other souls as their chief task. Giles Buckley, despising them, would nevertheless achieve a similar end by different means; a parlor advocate of communism (in his case indistinguishable from fascism), he would "make" everyone "do what is sensible and intelligent and right" (306). The two farcical characters, the beauticians, are found to have for some years suppressed their private problem of custodianship (although they are very much aware of their public mission); but it arises to confront them, and they are forced to "face up to" it in the funniest incident in the plot.

Of actual plot, the book has rather little, it is a "work of fiction" constructed of materials from the comedy of manners, the "anatomy," and the travelogue. The opening sentence introduces all three elements:

> Mrs. Richard Aubrey, the wife of a missionary bishop, sat outside the Café Bar Inaxion, in the Plaza de Armas, Fuenterrabia, one hot eighth of September, reconstructing, as was usual with her, the Garden of Eden. . . . While her husband . . . had striven to convert the uncultivated denizens of Mesopotamia, she, shyer, less fluent, much less convinced, and slightly unbalanced by the Mesopotamian sun, had ridden about on camels, donkeys, and other such creatures, brooding over that lost and lovely garden. . . . She had seen it in imagination as the various tale-tellers of Babylon and the East, and as the English poet Milton, had represented it, on who knows what grounds, to be. (7)

There follow two pages of her notes and queries, her Great Conversation with various ancient and medieval speculators as to the topography and horticulture of Eden and the race of its inhabitants, whom some had declared to be Basques. Her indefatigably donnish speculations are relevant to the various characters' sojourn in the Basque country: Mrs. Aubrey for the sake of research; the others, for a brief return to the Earthly Paradise—or to its substitute, this lovely coast. That Eden's "gardeners had got themselves into that pickle" (10) is the whole reason for the bishop's vocation and for the Groupers' Moral Re-Armament movement.

What there is of a plot consists chiefly in "resistance"—a holding action on the part of the other characters, who would like to continue calling their souls their own—pitted against the attempts of the Groupers to do them good. A parallel to this resistance is that of several of the characters to the beauticians' attempts to improve their appearance. The conflict between the Oxford Groupers and the Buckleys is over the custodianship of the soul of young Hero Buckley—a lovely but unhappy nineteen-year-old, somewhat backward intellectually, whose Byronic beauty charms every young man who sees her.

Hero's misery, which is made real enough, is nevertheless kept within reach of the comic spirit of the book; for it is shown to be caused partly by fear of death—an unlikely danger; and partly by a crush on an older, unattainable man. But she will be (and at last is) happier once her hopes are irrevocably dashed; furthermore, her nature is not one that can know profound tragedy. In this comedy of manners, Hero's mother might seem to be programmed for the *raisonneur;* she is graced with Rose Macaulay's favorite qualities—elegance, intelligence, calm, skepticism. By gentle raillery she tempers the authoritarianism and militarism represented by her son and husband—characters more or less limited to their humors. But her fastidious disinclination, arising from her nature and from her liberalism, to probe her daughter's unhappiness is not entirely appropriate to the situation.

Into the vacuum—the absence of spiritual shepherding—come the Groupers, who, despite their embarrassing excess of heartiness and their earnest gaucherie, which at first repel Hero, have comradeship to offer her. Ted Baines, their leader, undertakes "guidance"; managing to control any urge toward courtship, he becomes a firm friend and brings her to the confession that she so much needs to make to someone; and, finally—to the consternation of her parents—to a public avowal of her "Change." Much of this process is immature and funny, but the author clearly acknowledges some efficacy in it; Hero is considerably happier than she had been before. Under the guidance of the awkwardly honest Groupers—"absolute honesty" is one of their "four virtues" —Hero writes confessional letters of Total Recall to her parents, to her sister, and to the major whom she has so fruitlessly adored, "Sharing" all her guilty actions and thoughts in regard to them.

Her letter to her parents is read only in part by her humanly curious mother and not at all by her soldierly father, who holds that to partake of such intimate knowledge of another's soul would be unseemly. His wife muses: "I expect you're right. Not listening; not reading letters; changing the subject; looking the other way. I believe you have the key to all the difficulties of personal relationships . . ." (150). Their attitude leaves their daughter frustrated. Despairing of ever straightening out her filial relationship, she insists on being permitted to travel around for a time with the Groupers. She shares their views only in part, but some elements of their Changed way of life are necessary to her at this time to supplement the correct detachment of her parents and the estheticism of her brother Giles.

The comedy of manners includes conflict arising not only from differences of taste and principles but also from those of age and worldly experiences. The bishop hopes that "absolute honesty" will not prove too discouraging to those young people who attempt it; Sir Arthur thinks of it as a possible technique for revenge, but doubts that the satisfaction would be worth the breach of civility.

The worst victims of the "anatomy" are not the Oxford Groupers but the Josefs, the beauticians. Rose Macaulay harbored no objections to facial fantasy, as she had made clear in *What Not*. But she considered beauticians quacks and their propaganda inimical to a sane scheme of values. Unfortunately, in *Going Abroad* the anatomizing of the procedures used by the Josefs in their beauty culture involves the listing of many details so exaggerated that the reader's reaction tends less toward amusement than rebellion. It is the beauticians' farcical parallel to the Groupers that is very funny.

Halfway through the book, the mild conflicts that have so far characterized it are suddenly exchanged for comic melodrama. The Josefs, whose business would have been embarrassed by the presence of their incurably ugly daughters, have exiled these girls to the grandparents' peasant home high in the Pyrenees. None of the mountain Basque youths will marry such ugly girls without the dowry that their wealthy parents ought to provide. On a scenic bus ride to the shrine of that disciplined saint, Loyola, the vacationers find themselves kidnapped by the girls' guardians. This peripety brings together with new interactions the comedy of manners, the travelogue, and the anatomy.

Night in the mountain corral, where "a few had to be content with piles of dry leaves and moss," gives an ethical challenge promptly taken up by the Groupers, eager for martyrdom; the disciplined colonel; and the "unselfish, though rheumatic bishop" (196). Custodianship appears in new forms. Before retiring, the Basques, now termed "hosts," decide to prevent the escape of the "guests" by putting them on parole; their word of honor, however, will not do: the Anglicans and Groupers must swear "on the crucifix of Señor Felix Mendizobal"—one of their captors and the intended of the younger Josef girl, if she receives her dowry. While the colonel, strong in his sense of the Empire's custodianship of its subjects, plans legal redress, the cheerful Basque kidnappers are lying around the fire, "content in the knowledge that they had done, and were doing, their duty" (197-98).

Several funny passages arise from Mrs. Aubrey's study of the Basque language, in which many words differ only slightly from words of quite another meaning. These confusions reach their climax during the captivity, when the idealistic lady thinks she hears them speaking of religion, revolution, the ancient laws, and autonomy. But it seems that the conversation was about "brandy," "silk," "lace," and "not enough money" (212-13). The word for smuggling is not included in the Basque-Spanish dictionary, and Ted comments: ". . . it rather shows the people haven't faced up to it, doesn't it?" "There are in all dictionaries," said Sir Arthur, "only too many gaps where words they haven't faced up to should be. Even the Oxford . . ." (186-87).

Finally the local priest appears; and the three scholars, having little Basque, while he has retained little of his school Spanish, try to communicate with him in Latin. Each delivers some formidable passage on freedom that he recalls from school or university. Guessing that the strangers are reciting some holy Latin text, the priest politely responds each time, "Ita est" (218-20). More effectively, the Group girls, relentlessly plying Mme Josef —who is imprisoned in the henhouse—with talk of sin and duty, bring her to such an emotional pitch that she agrees to sign the check for the dowry.

Back in the sea again at Zarauz, Mrs. Buckley is trying to win her son Giles away from his narrow esthetic views (he has just scorned the Groupers for calling each other "pals"): ". . . *is* any one of the ways in which humanity behaves inherently more ridiculous than the others?" Spluttering in the waves, he mocks:

"And isn't there good in everything, and should we not try to find it, and be more ready to approve than to condemn? Your generation has no . . . standards. . . . The shoal of pals . . . and I . . . at least . . . have those . . ." (310-11). Giles's formulation of the split between liberalism and totalitarianism and his perception of which side the Moral Re-Armament movement tended toward was borne out later in the 1930's when it gave signs of approving Nazism. Rose Macaulay, though skeptical of the percipience of individuals, was more skeptical of the wisdom of dictators (for her journalism on this topic, see ch. V, sec. 7).

Resting in Cambridge before returning to his mission diocese, the bishop is back at work on his *Early Christian Heresies as Exemplified among Modern Primitive Men.* He thinks of the Collyridians, the Eustachians, the Waldensians, Fraticelli, Dulcinists, with their strange enthusiasms and taboos; the Manicheeans, Gnostics, and many others "so harshly disapproved of and condemned"; and, finally, of the Groupers, "working away, with such comradely helpfulness and confidence, at the lives of the Basques, adjuring them to come clean, to renounce kidnapping, smuggling and tobacco. . . ." Despite the anticlimax that the author has slipped into this sequence, the bishop cannot let himself agree with Sir Arthur that life may be "a rather absurd comic film" (314-16).

I Would Be Private (1937), an entertaining but minor novel, which includes a delightful, self-contained young Scottish policeman and his quintuplets, will be omitted from this discussion for reasons of space.

VI   The Writings of E. M. Forster

Early in 1938 the Hogarth Press published Rose Macaulay's *The Writings of E. M. Forster,* the first book of criticism to be devoted to this writer. As a critic of Forster, Rose Macaulay was privileged: two years younger than he, she belonged to his "generation"; they were both members of the "intellectual aristocracy" (ch. I, sec. 1); they had both spent impressionable years in Cambridge; they were both well acquainted with Italy and Greece; they were both novelists and journalists; and they were friends.

Rose Macaulay's method is to take Forster's integrity as a man and as an author as her central fact; she describes the social milieu that had its part in shaping him, but she makes no attempt to subject him to a psychological analysis, or to use the works biographically–except as they bear witness to his widening experience and gradually altering views.

The writings of Forster and Rose Macaulay are sufficiently similar for her comments to be of great interest in relation to her own career as an author. "He would agree," she suggests, "with Anatole France, that Irony and Pity should be the witnesses and the judges of human life"; and she notes that Forster "commanded their services at an age"–she refers to an essay he published at twenty-four–"when most other writers have not yet learnt to use them." This statement might have been made of her own *Abbots Verney,* published when she was twenty-five; and also her further comment: "In this exquisite brief essay you will find all the charm, the humour, the gay, gentle mocking flexibility of rhythm, almost every characteristic turn of style, that you will find in essays . . . thirty years later" (23-24). Both writers in their early works imagined too wide a gap between the university and the outside world; Rose Macaulay found in *The Longest Journey* certain "signs of adolescence . . . . Cambridge, being too near, is too golden a Utopia, too alma a mater" (62).

In each novel Forster has experimented with a different "key" to "the odd riddle with which we are posed": "In *Where Angels Fear to Tread,* the contrast is between the direct, pagan joy in life, and drab conventional propriety. In *The Longest Journey* it is between honesty and muddled meanness; in *A Room with a View* between real feeling and pretended; the darkness is the darkness of sham. . . . But in *Howards End* the darkness is that of inhuman depersonalization, the refusal to accept the implications of personal intercourse" (123-24). In *A Passage to India* "the personal relationship, which in *Howards End* is to be the general solvent, is here less inadequate than irrelevant . . ." (199). Thus, Forster is seen as a man–a man thinking and intuiting, and then weighing and sharing what he has found.

When this communicating takes the form of the novel, which imposes upon thought certain esthetic requirements of its own, so that Forster asks us to repeat with him "a little sadly. . . . Yes–oh, dear, yes–the novel tells a story,'" Rose Macaulay suspects that there will be a large school of readers who instead will "cry joyfully, 'Yes, thank God, it does. Thank God for the enthralling stories of *Howards End, A Passage to India, A Room with a View, The Longest Journey'* . . ." (230-31). But she admits that Forster sometimes lets the needs of the plot distort the characters.

In his first novel, *Where Angels Fear to Tread,* Forster proved the power of his creative imagination in the characters of the Italian Gino and his English wife Lilia—characters from "an uncultivated stratum of alien social life." Of a conversation between young Italian men she says: "Translate this into Italian"—a language she had known well since childhood—"and see how right it reads." In this novel Forster was less successful with the two young women from his own milieu—"foolish (I fear incredible) Caroline Abbott, disagreeable (I hope incredible) Harriet . . ." (38-40); but the objective portrait of Agnes in *The Longest Journey* and the objective and subjective presentation of Lucy in *A Room with a View* demonstrate his increasing sophistication in depicting women. As for Lucy's persistent rejection of George's love, it seems an unfortunate distortion imposed by the needs of the plot.

To Margaret Schlegel, of *Howards End,* Forster gave "most of the attributes that please civilized women in one another. Beauty, merely feminine charm, single-track emotion, biological urge—these qualities, so confusing and swamping to personality and character, so much the stock-in-trade of the heroine-maker, in Margaret Schlegel scarcely exist; in consequence we see her as an individual, with mind, heart, intelligence, sympathies, theories, and ideas" (107). By the time he depicted the Schlegel sisters his "experience of life" had reached "a stage from which he could tackle women as freely, as many-sidedly . . . as he could tackle men; that is to say, he could tackle their minds as well as their emotions." Few writers of either sex can do this with the other; "a certain sexless, or epicene, quality seems to be required for it" (115). Finally, Adela, in *A Passage to India,* "is a type belonging less to fiction than to life; everything about her is true; unromantic realist, with no appeal beyond that of youth, integrity, and a civilized mind, she is a heroine rare in novels" (191).

As for the men, Rose Macaulay questions the plausibility of Rickie's tragic horror at the idea that his hated father had sired an illegitimate son: ". . . in one brought up to the habits of the Greek gods, so strong a reaction" was unlikely "to a not, after all, surprising or very shocking fact" (56). Throughout her critique, in pointing out her friend's faults, she invokes the spirit of comedy. After indicating several examples of faulty character portrayal–Cecil Vyse, Mr. Beebe, Ronny Heaslop–she finds that Aziz in *A Passage to India* "is a brilliantly drawn figure, more living than any of the Englishmen; an extraordinary tour-de-force in the portraiture of one race by another" (194).

Frequently in her book Rose Macaulay calls attention to Forster's remarkable command of idiom–his own as narrator and that of his characters.[8] In *A Passage to India* the opening conversation between Aziz, Hamidullah, and Mahmoud Ali "has an air of the most convincing authenticity. This writing by an Englishman about a social gathering of three Mohammedan Indians is a feat which must, if we remember other such gatherings described by other English writers, dazzle us by its sheer virtuosity" (195). In *Howards End* "no sentence uttered by either" of the sisters "could be mistaken for the other's" (114). He succeeds, too, with the inarticulate and the silly. In *The Longest Journey,* "the humour throughout is a mixture of ironic slant and comment, and of the more extroverted wit that reveals itself in the uncommented conversations of the characters" (64); this statement would be an equally accurate description of her own writing.

Forster, she finds, became expert at perceiving the phenomenal and interpreting it in terms of the noumenal (23). Early in the century, she points out, "fiction had a fashion of Maeterlinckian moral generalizations which would be disconcerting today. . ." (as in her *Secret River*). In *A Room with a View* "it is naturally, not the spiritual battles, not truth nor Eros nor Pallas Athene, that hold our interest . . . ; I can even imagine being bored by these sublime beings and their wrestlings" (83). But *Howards End,* his "first fully adult book," is "richly packed with meanings; it has a mellow brilliance, a kind of shot beauty of texture; it runs like a bright, slowish, flickering river, in which different kinds of exciting fish swim and dart among mysterious reedy depths and are observed and described by a highly interested, humane, sympathetic, often compassionate, and usually ironic commentator" (100).

His history of Alexandria is "most agreeable reading, full of scholarship, spirit, poetry, humour and prejudices"–or of "strong tastes and distastes. Mr. Forster, a Hellenist, humanist, and anti-medievalist . . . deplores the dark and barbarous centuries" that engulfed the culture he admires. She finds that, in his description of a certain Alexandrian theological quarrel as " 'this arid theological Odyssey,' his sympathies seem imperfect, his imagination unduly depressed by classical and humanist distaste, for there was nothing that fourth-century Alexandrians enjoyed more than a first-class theological scrap, and it is apparent that a capital time was had by all" (137-39).

The portraits in his literary essays "have a delicate and springing life . . . ." And she asks, is the novelist "perhaps the permanent leader of Mr. Forster's writing team?" In the 1920's he wrote only one novel, "but the novelist is busy through nearly all the literary criticism, articles, and essays, even the most casual of current reviews, making portraits and characters . . ." (220-21).

Although he was apt to be unfair, she thought, to clergymen, schoolmasters, scientists, and–as he grew more leftist–perhaps to "Them" ("Them . . . who govern us"), in his reviews he was very kind. In dealing with books good and less good, "he brings a felicity of judgment and of phrase that is not satire, scarcely even irony . . ." (212). In fact, "his sympathies are with the people underneath, behind and outside the right places and the right clubs. . . . He prefers the eccentric . . ." (206).

Rose Macaulay judges *Aspects of the Novel* an "uneven" book; and, as in a gay debate at a party, she discovers flaws in point after point in her friend's disquisition. His theorizing on plot is "more chatty than coherent . . . ." She rebels against his debasing "that fine word" *curiosity* by "divorcing it from intelligence" (238). As for "this question of flatness and roundness," it is "debatable, subjective, and complicated," as is "apparent whenever novels and people in them are discussed among a group of intelligent readers" (235-36). His "extension of the limits of fantasy might have been carried to further lengths; there is a fantastic element in a great deal of 'straight fiction' which might have been touched on, for it is a subject particularly suited to the lecturer" (239-40)–and particularly of interest, it might be observed, to his critic. She is dubious about the pamphlet *Anonym-*

ity. An Enquiry: "Mr. Forster, as a poet and mystic, comes down on one side; as stylist and individualist, he might likely enough, on some other occasion, take the other" (224).

His articles in the 1920's and 1930's on the state of the world and on the menace of war lack his special cachet; they could have been written by "some other intelligent, rational and sensitive writer. Probably because his usual style, however seriously he is writing, is largely compact of humour, fancy, and allusiveness, and these dark and grim subjects give little scope for such graces" (225). No doubt Rose Macaulay's own similar writing at this time made her uneasily aware of the equal unsatisfactoriness of renouncing one's special style and of using it inappropriately.

She sets down Forster's "root beliefs"–beliefs that are the foundation of her own work, although it pleased her to subject them to skeptical review: "in the permanent value and importance of human beings, and perhaps"–for he, too, was skeptical–"of their relationships with one another; . . . in culture, that can understand and receive beauty; . . . in freedom, intellectual, social, and personal" (270-71). Because his esthetic emphasis "includes the whole of life, it is never 'arty'; he is every time with the simple philistine against the pretentious cultured; and because it is witty it is never either empurpled or remote" (294). And she declares: "I do not know where the *charged* effect of his prose is to be paralleled in English fiction, except in some of the prose of Virginia Woolf, and here and there in D. H. Lawrence's. . . . it suggests such pressure of thought and meaning on language that no word or phrase is empty, and nothing said or done by any of his creatures is idle" (274).

Rose Macaulay's critique follows the method used by Forster in his reviewing; her judgments are not "institutional and referred" but have "the immediacy of personal taste." It may be added that they are also, strikingly, characterized by the immediacy of personal knowledge of the world. She finds that "the English method" of criticism, as contrasted with the French, is based on "feeling that [the works] are enough in themselves, without comparing them with what they ought to be." She considers Forster's work in itself, and the faults that she finds are measured in terms of his own proved potential and not in terms of some criterion foreign to his genius. In her critique, as in his reviews, "zest and penetration go hand in hand, and wit flatters the reader into borrowed discernment . . ." (212-13). Wit is also kind to her subject's errors: the book is urbane, but lively; loyal, but frank. Her fault-finding is transmuted into gentle irony, or astonishment, or gay bantering. For she never doubts the essential soundness of the rock on which Forster's writings are founded. That rock is also of precious stone–of its glinting, she gives her impressions in delightful metaphors. But she follows these up with exact analytical terms. For the first full-length presentation of an author, the book seems extremely well conceived.

VII *Journalism*

Rose Macaulay's very extensive journalism in the 1930's was concerned with literature–among her articles in this field were an evaluation of Coventry Patmore (*New Statesman and Nation,* I [March 29, 1931], v-vi) and a chapter on John Lyly and Sir Philip Sidney in a "survey of the novel by twenty contemporary novelists"[9]–but even more with general subjects. With Forster and other "Bloomsbury" figures, she shared the sense of responsibility for encouraging the play of ideas–in fact, playfulness with ideas–and for contributing enlightened comment to guide the thinking of those less well endowed and less well educated. As a result, her discussions involve a great variety of topics. Sometimes she is moved to speak sharply, sometimes bitterly; but almost invariably she finishes her article with a return to some degrees of skepticism, kindness, and ebullient humor. Occasionally she writes in the mischievous tone of demure naïveté used in some of the essays in *A Casual Commentary.*

Most of her sixty-odd weekly columns in *Spectator* in 1935 and 1936 discuss more than one topic, but a notion of her scope can be gained from a sketchy listing from the spring of 1935: belligerence arising between critics of arts, literature, etc.; differences of pronunciation; censorship; Lord's Day Observance Society and people's preference for sports and love; the language of invective; Abyssinia and the warring Europeans; shamelessness of press in invading bereavement; intercession in foreign wrongs to other foreign nations; if English of past centuries are called "Tudors," "Stuarts," etc., we must be "Guelphs"; police cars and speed limits

–lock step; youth looks ahead; girls' colleges; contemporary books; peace conferences; geo-studies; humanity has always been in a parlous plight; the law against sleeping outdoors in fields, etc.; libel; if all novels were altered to bring the objects and diction up to date; ignorance of other people's terms; names of social groups; book thefts.

In "What I Believe," in 1931, she had called "ignorance, vulgarity, and cruelty" "the three black jungle horrors" (*Nation*, CXXXIII [December 16, 1931], 665). She was concerned about Mosley's anti-Semitism, about the troubles in Spain, and, always, about tyrannical aspects of government at home and elsewhere. The present writer has read some hundred and fifty of her articles in various papers and journals; few are disappointing; many deserve collection. A memorable one is "Full Fathom Five," a serio-comic "Auto-Obituary" (ch. IV, sec. 1) which tells of her death in a flying accident at the age of one hundred and two. This saturnine evaluation of her character and work ends: "there sinks an old lady of no great talent, but who managed, on the whole, to put in a pretty good time."

In the last years of the decade she joined in the efforts to avert a general war. She wrote an Introduction and gave some assistance to Daniel George Bunting toward the compiling of *All in a Maze* (London: Collins, 1938), a book that included brief excerpts from writings or utterances on peace and the dreadfulness of war, in chronological order from Aeschylus to Neville Chamberlain. In her Introduction she says: "Then entered the Christians, striking a new note of moral and religious pacifism, which was not sustained after Christianity became the imperial creed. . . . To the humane intellectual civility of Erasmus, war was an insanity . . ." (8-9). In *An Open Letter to a Non-Pacifist* (London: The Peace Pledge Union, 1937) she distinguishes between sane and hysterical pacifism, and does not minimize the difficulties of "mass non-violent resistance" (not to be confused with non-resistance).[10] She refutes the argument that citizens accepting the protection of the State must also accept, "without protest, the conditions and circumstances of this protection." Would her opponent support this view for citizens of dictatorships? For ancestors who might have protested against torturing traitors and burning witches? (6-7).

VIII   And No Man's Wit

And No Man's Wit was written during the autumn that followed the final defeat, in March, 1939, of the Republican forces
in the Spanish Civil War. The story–which takes place in Spain
that summer and ends with the mobilization of England and
France momentarily expected for the stand against the Nazis–
concerns Dr. Kate Marlowe's search through the exhausted Iberian provinces for her son Guy, a volunteer in the International
Brigade, who may still be alive there somewhere. With her in a
little car are her other son, Hugh–dogmatically Communist; her
daughter Betsey, who lives democracy but refuses to bother
theorizing about it or demonstrating for it; a young mechanic,
Ernie, one of Guy's associates in the Brigade; and slim, blonde,
but strangely other-worldly Ellen Green. Their visit on the estate
of a young Aragonese nobleman, an Oxford friend of Guy's, the
Marqués Ramón del Monte, where they meet his family and his
friend Armand, the son of a wealthy French manufacturer,
amounts to a *cena* (see ch. II, n. 9), at which conversations–
some of them heated–are engendered on several different lines
of political belief.

When the book was published, in June, 1940, its readers were
being bombed in the Battle of Britain. The reviewer for the *Times
Literary Supplement* (June 22, 1940, 301) was troubled by the
choice of this subject for an exercise of "the disinterested imagination," but he granted that "she writes with sincerity and courage
and from a full and evidently considered knowledge of Spanish
history." But surely the time when the book was in process–the
months of the "phony war," when there was still hope of averting
the threatened holocaust–was an appropriate time to point out
the human wastage that inevitably results from extremisms, from
partial-sighted human beings trying to settle matters of belief in a
"life and death" (the reviewer's words) frame of mind. In these
chaotic mid-century conditions, "The Sun is lost, and the earth,
and no man's wit/ Can well direct him where to look for it"
(Donne, "An Anatomie of the World," 1611).

The incidents in the novel are minor rather than major–irrita-
tions flaring up, hinderings, contests over small matters that sym-
bolize great ones in the minds of the opponents, petty revenges–

the microcosmic forms of the inter-class, inter-party, and international oppositions that divide the characters. But the macrocosm is always equally present as the characters thrash out their views and recall what these have implied in distant and recent historical events.

The "sharply characterized individuals" who dwell in, or travel across, "tragic immemorial Spain" (*New York Times Book Review*, October 27, 1940, 6) constitute, as the *Times* reviewer observed, "a team after Miss Macaulay's heart." Dr. Marlowe is a liberal—busy even in Spain sending telegrams to influence the course of events in one place or another. Though the author herself shared in this activity, she saw it as somewhat comic: sometimes one asks oneself "with some mistrust, what have I today abolished, what preserved? . . . Can I, in some absent moment, have abolished Abyssinia and protected Cruel Sports? . . . Indeed, . . . all abolition and all protection Societies are ['for the Abolition of Human Nature']" (*Spectator*, CLXIV [May 22, 1936], 929). On the del Monte estate are the "vieja marquesa," a worldly, perspicacious old lady, once of the Court group; the marquesa, Ramón's widowed mother, of narrow understanding and sympathies, a Churchly fanatic and a Carlist; Ramón, a modern young man who nevertheless adheres to the proud traditional autonomy of the Aragón nobleman; and his fine, proud young sister, Antonia, impassioned over the "Hispanidad" project to recover her nation's lost empire.

The hundred pages devoted to the offerings, rejections, and partial acceptances of friendship and the empty intellectual triumphs that make up the social comedy, with pathos, of the Marlowes' overnight visit at the manor compose a brilliant complex of thought and expression. The heedless sincerity of Betsey appears ridiculous to the formal Aragonese; but their faces do not betray this reaction as they greet her politely (35). The del Montes easily manage to ignore Ernie (who had been foraging on the estate during the war—an experience that he makes memorable in a superb nonsequitur: they found the wall "proper spikey" and topped with broken glass—"so over we got . . ." [19]). Ramón never fails in politeness to his bigoted mother and never concedes anything to her in his behavior. The English gradually become aware of the great diversity of allegiance among Spanish conservatives. The del Montes scorn Franco as an upstart; individually, they are disappointed in his failure to reestablish Alfonso's line or the Carlist line, or the feudal power of the medieval states, or the Spanish Empire, or the full power of the Church. Which was "the true Spain" for whose sake all were fighting, including the International Brigade?

The several del Montes interpret differently their adherence to the Church. Betsey, to please Ellen, had removed a cheap plaster statue of a saint that stood above their bed and, slipping, had dropped it. She manfully confesses her fault and apologizes, ending with, "We were going to put her in the wardrobe." While the Frenchman urbanely murmurs, "As if the poor saint were a ticking clock . . .," the marquesa begins a series of frigidly ironic observations. Ramón, with complete politeness, quickly manages to voice his own opinion of ill-considered pieties and to transform his mother's sarcastic words into a wise judgment: "Perhaps on the other hand Miss Green has a taste very fine, and does not like painted plaster. But, as you say, mama, it's of no consequence whatever" (70-71). Dr. Marlowe, less deft, scores a point against her hostess; but she does so at the expense of rudeness: " 'One understands,' said the Englishwoman, rather red, 'that [Franco] intends to model the new Spain on the new Germany—Gestapo, gleichgeschaltet press, concentration camps, and all. In fact he is obviously doing so. Though I suppose, as your Jews were disposed of in former centuries, you can't have the complete Nazi system here" (82).

The grandmother, the vieja marquesa, believes—like the rich French bourgeois, Armand—in a rigid social structure without repression or prudery. (Her free viewing of life has enabled her to be the one who correctly guesses Guy's present circumstances.) She doubts that Spanish politics will ever be peaceful. Her talk and the Marlowes' subsequent experiences with bureaucracy bring Dr. Marlowe to a feeling of despair: "Each day, as Spain's strange, illiberal impenetrability daunted her a little more, she sank into a drearier scepticism, not only as to finding Guy, but as to the very foundations of her faith and his, the roots from which their life sprang. . . . Spain was a cenotaph of lost causes and slain hopes: its parched plains, rocky peaks, lean flocks, high-walled cities, clanging bells, inscrutable olive faces, mocked the

stranger . . ." (210). A couple of nights later, however, Ramón
has recognized Guy among a troop of gypsies and is secretly aid-
ing the old friend whom he considers an "invader." He also is
scheming with his age-mate to postpone any announcement to Dr.
Marlowe for a time, as he would like to travel a few weeks longer
with Ellen. Spain gives other proofs of kindliness. Guy, for whose
capture the police are offering a reward, finally leaves his gypsy
mistress and makes for the French border with the help of a
Basque smuggler. As he and some others are crossing the last
stream, guards open fire; when two men are felled, a young
Spanish priest turns back to stay with his captured compatriots.

An element all but irrelevant to these problems is the mystery
of Ellen Green, for the pleasure of whose lovely but baffling company Ramón undertakes to travel with the Marlowes in their
search. She is part mermaid. During the last swim of the Marlowe
party, Ellen turns from those who are calling her on the shore of
that dusty land, and, in seven of Rose Macaulay's most delightful
pages, swims away into the Mediterranean and down into its
depths—"flat round forms sailed by, like shadows of plates; from
the foremost end of one of them two eyes shot up on stalks and
goggled at Ellen; a purple oval form hoisted a sail in front and
sped by like a boat . . . . Radiant, transparent, jellied beings
drifted by like moons . . . . galaxies of little luminous fish, can-
dling the purple depths with their faint glow. . . . Dim shapes
rose and sank about her, finning stealthily on their way"—until, in
the night, suddenly panic seizes her, and, not entirely a mermaid,
the lovely naked girl cries for help and drowns (324-29).[11]

The salt-water world of the sea, from which the human race
came, is a world of preying, fear, and personal solitude. In the
human world, in spite of wars, man can achieve decency and love
in personal relations. At the end of the book, Guy, wounded and
in gypsy rags, sits at a table across the border in France accepting
assistance from his political opponents Armand and Ramón. They
discuss, in easy fellowship, their sharply differing views: "It is
people that matter, Guy thought. One can differ about anything
and still sit and talk" (383).

Guy represents his creator's view when he says, "My petty
princedom would be built on respect for individuals. It would be
the very opposite of these damned corporate states which despise

and fear and suppress the individual" (381). But, as Armand and Ramón heckle him, his creator's skepticism also appears–her doubts about the value of the ordinary man's thought; and her doubt that zeal–even liberal zeal–can long refrain from stiffening itself into tyranny, as the marquesa's Carlism adds its bigotry to her natural stupidity and noble little Antonia's "Hispanidad" prevents her from entering into sympathetic relations with friendly Betsey, whose country holds Gibraltar.

When the book ends, the Russians have made their treaty with the Germans, and World War II is about to begin. Guy will go to fight against the Nazis, as will Armand, but from different principles. Dr. Marlowe's misery at this time reflects the author's feelings (as indicated in S) during the confused weeks of the summer and autumn of 1939:

> Oh, what does one mean by pacifist? I think war is horrible and cruel and grotesque, of course, and belongs to the dark ages as much as the rack and thumbscrew do. But if you ask me, is nothing worse, I think it's worse to let more and more people be tortured and enslaved without protest–I mean, effective protest. On the other hand, *is* war the only way to stop it, and have we tried all the others? Of course we haven't. . . . It would be simpler if one could be wholly pacifist. But the pacifists don't seem to have alternate ways to suggest of stopping the Nazis. And they *are* sometimes very silly. (315-16)

Dr. Marlowe is one of Rose Macaulay's best "natural" characters; she is very fully seen. In her are exhibited the strengths and limitations of the enlightened liberal. She mothers her children, but on principle takes care not to interfere. She has enough sense to value social decorum, but she recognizes it as a procedure, not an end. She devotes herself to setting the world right, yet suffers from agonizing doubts. Before some aspects of life, she remains naïve: elegance of deportment, impersonal gaiety, the cold self-regarding virtues. But her effort toward a large wisdom enables the author to move easily, in her company, from the phenomenal to the noumenal.

CHAPTER 6

Travel-History, Journalism, and Fiction, 1942-1958

I Wartime Experiences

DESPITE her abhorrence of war and her feeling, in the first months of World War II, that something might still be done to avert its continuance, Rose Macaulay immediately became active, driving her little Morris car for an Ambulance Station. Even when the bombing began, "she met its impact with her usual capacity to find enjoyment in almost everything. . . . All in all, the surge of events during the first eighteen months of the war brought more stimulation than distress" to her (S, 20-21). In September, 1940 she commented on the ambulance men: "They are very nice and matey. I like their way of calling everyone (including the ambulance women) 'mate'" (S, 114). The neighborhood where she lived, and which she would not leave, was often bombed, being between two clusters of railway stations. Then, in May, 1941, her own apartment and her fifteeen hundred books, her notes and papers—nearly all her belongings—were destroyed (see ch. V, n. 1); the next winter she became ill; and in the summer of 1942 the man she loved died. The effect of these events appeared in her two final novels; but, until some time after the war, she could not bring herself to attempt fiction, although she worked steadily—through a sequence of illnesses—at other writing.

In 1941-42 Collins published a series of over a hundred thin books, with period illustrations, under the general title "Britain in Pictures." The texts were written by eminent persons. Each subject was treated historically, but the tone tended to be one of pride. The purpose would seem to have been to provide attractive "conversation-pieces" that would strengthen the British in their belief in the nation they were defending. Of these books,

Life among the English (1942) was written by Rose Macaulay. It begins with the Britons and the Roman colonists and carries through until the time of writing. The tone, however, is seldom one of pride; frequently the author is having great fun–the book is extremely entertaining. Some of the time she is offering a straight historical redaction; much of the time she is mildly derisive; concerning some phases of history, she can but be bitter. Taking its place in the series, her book implies, "Let us, at least, not be hypocritical."

The twentieth century is passed over hastily–shrugged off, perhaps; for in 1942, many of its vaunted improvements were seen to have been impermanent. The end of the 1930's could be treated only with bitter humor and wry allusion: soon after the Munich conference "many new fashions came in; windows were crisscrossed with tape; gas masks were carried about and left in cinemas and on blackberry bushes . . ." (47). With the bombing raids and the rationing, class distinctions were in abeyance: "English social life is, in these curious, dark, troubled years, moving a few steps nearer that democracy for which we say we are fighting and have never yet had. Only a few steps; and whether these will be retraced or continued when the solvent furnace of war dies down, and we are left to grope a way through wreckage and smouldering ashes, we cannot yet know" (48).

In 1945 and 1946 Rose Macaulay wrote monthly assessments of the B.B.C. radio programs for *Time and Tide*. In the review that covered May, 1945, she attacked the "sneering cacaphony" of the radio music chosen for VE Day as "an affront . . . to the . . . slain, maimed and bitterly bereaved, an affront . . . to tortured Europe. . . ." The speeches included "too much self-praise, 'You did not flinch,' etc. But of course we flinched. Why not? One gets tired of this myth of absolute fearlessness that we are building up about ourselves . . . . We also black-marketed, and looted bombed houses" (XXVI [June 2, 1945], 454).

Rose Macaulay was one of a group of writers who paid homage to Virginia Woolf, just after her death, in the May, 1941, issue of *Horizon* (III, 316-18). Her tribute generously evokes the vivid personality of her friend. Her article in *Spectator,* directed more toward the works, finds that their "supreme interest" results from the "interflow of the outward and the inward" (CLXVI [April 11, 1941], 394).

II They Went to Portugal

Rose Macaulay's interest in the Iberian peninsula resulted in two other books, *They Went to Portugal* (1946) and *Fabled Shore: from the Pyrenees to Portugal* (1949). *They Went to Portugal,* which she set herself to working at after the personal disasters of the first years of the war, "entailed a good deal of hard work and research" in London and in Lisbon, which she visited in 1943 (*L,* 116). The book contains thirty-six accounts of British persons, or groups of persons, who went to Portugal, from the time of the Crusades through the nineteenth century. They are grouped in such categories as royalty, writers, clergymen, port wine merchants, tourists, interventionists, plotters, ambassadors. In each case, the author vivifies her account with quotations from her subject's letters or diaries and from the comments of contemporaries–if possible, both British and Portuguese. Rose Macaulay's erudition, together with her accustomed sense of the ironic and her ability to sympathize with many different patterns of life, enabled her to see each visitor–intent as he was upon his own purposes and limited by his habitual frame of reference–as part of a broad whole.

An enthusiast for "abroad," she leads her readers, by her witty devices, toward a wider tolerance. Among the clergymen, one of the founders of Methodism, George Whitefield, reported that he used his ship's call at Lisbon to "see something of the superstitions of the Church of Rome." On the road from his port to Lisbon, Rose Macaulay observes, "he looked about him, and what he saw was not the Tagus, nor the Jeronimos, nor palaces, orange gardens, churches and gaily coloured houses, nor even the Portuguese women going about their business driving donkeys and carrying loads on their heads"; he saw only "wayside shrines" and people "bowing to them and singing"–aspects of religion that seemed to him "very odd" (204-5). A year later came the earthquake, which he saw as a divine judgment; she comments, "Less than twenty years later Mr. Whitefield's own Bethesda College was destroyed by fire" (206).

Robert Southey, on a visit in 1795, was horrified by Iberian inns: "for a youth of twenty-one, afire with republican principles and dreams of founding a Utopia in an American wilderness, he was definitely fussy about discomfort, dirt, hard beds, insects, and smells" (144). Of a different mettle was the Reverend J. M. Neale, a militant High Churchman, who went to Portugal in 1853: "He had not wrestled with persecuting bishops in Sussex to be overthrown by vermin and bad lodging in Portugal. . . . However weary, however languid, however sore distressed, he would always struggle on. . . . any bodily fatigues and bodily anguish were turned to joy by the mountain views of the Minho and Tras-os-Montes, even on muleback in the rain."[1]

The author is aware, however, that some visitors had met with more serious hazards. In 1550 George Buchanan, a Scottish Catholic overly influenced by the humanism of Erasmus, was suddenly seized, while teaching upon invitation at a college in Coimbra, and delivered to the Inquisition. By responding with extreme artfulness, he was eventually given a lenient sentence, which "showed that his judges had tried to be just"; but the rest of his life must have been haunted by "memories of that dreadful year in a dungeon cell of the Holy House in the Rocio, when days and weeks of comfortless and solitary fear had been punctuated only by terrific, incriminating, trapping interrogations before seven quiet, nagging, patient, evidence-primed judges and a scribbling notary in the corner; when questions, sometimes silly, sometimes alarmingly to the point, had been shot at him in the bigoted, nasal voice of men who tortured and burnt . . ." (76).

William Beckford, on the other hand, the wealthy eighteenth-century esthete, met with nothing worse than the social embargo which the English court had ordered the English ambassador to observe. He had had to seek a foreign home "since his own country hissed and tittered with scandal about him." Although rebuffed by his compatriots, he was accepted by the best Portuguese society. While the great Marialva family sought to arrange a match between him and "the lovely bastard Henriqueta," he made entries in his diary about the adoration offered him by the Marquis' fifteen-year-old son (110-13).

Despite the objections that Rose Macaulay had to some aspects of Roman Catholicism—infallibility, prohibition of intercommunion ("When we were little girls going to the daily convent school at Varazze for a time, the nuns wouldn't even let us join in prayers with the other children; we had to sit down, lest the awful sin

should be committed of praying with little heretics." [*L*, 322, 341]
–there were other aspects toward which she was very friendly.
She describes a pleasant enclave in Lisbon, "the English Nun-
nery," a community of Bridgettine nuns who had fled to Portugal
in 1594:

> British sailors frequented the convent grille, for sweetmeats and
> chat, with such assiduity that, in 1735, when the British fleet lay
> in the Tagus for a year, the lady abbess had to ration their visits;
> and during the Peninsular War a group of English protestant sail-
> ors, having observed that the Syon Convent monstrance was infe-
> rior to others in Lisbon churches, 'exclaimed with an oath that
> their countrywomen should have as fine a house for their God as
> the Portuguese', and subscribed among themselves for a very
> handsome monstrance, which the sisters use to this day. (267)

As the *Times Literary Supplement* reviewer observed, at the
end of a full-page review, *They Went to Portugal* is "a book to
be read and re-read" (November 9, 1946, 548).

III Fabled Shore

Fabled Shore (1949)[2] is the account of a trip–an "expedition,"
one might almost call it–that Rose Macaulay made two years after
World War II at the age of sixty-six, alone in a little pre-war
Morris car, on the poorly paved (sometimes unpaved) roads
along the entire Mediterranean coast of Spain and on to Cap
Vincente in Portugal. In those days there was almost no tourism
on what the *Times Literary Supplement* reviewer called "this un-
frequented coast," and virtually no Spaniards had ever seen a
woman drive a car. "Her book," the reviewer declared, "puts Miss
Macaulay in that select group of British originals whose travel
stories are peculiar to our literature" (May 6, 1949, 291).

Harold Nicolson, devoting his weekly review in the *Observer*
to it, asked: "What is it that makes a good book of travel? The
difficult gift . . . of imparting enjoyment. . . . the capacity of im-
plying, rather than of imposing, the beauty of the works of God
and man. A certain sense of historical perspective, an ability to
convey information without being prosaic, a style variable enough
to carry a continuous narrative without monotony, average powers

of observation and interpretation, and marked eccentricity on the part of the author. Rose Macaulay possesses each of these qualities" (May 1, 1949, 7).

The elements of "eccentricity" are found in what might be called the "coordinates" that determine the field of her book: her constant search for good places to swim ("bathe") and for architectural evidences of the successive waves of human civilizations that have established themselves along these coasts. In *And No Man's Wit* she had taken her turn among those who have written of what Cyril Connolly called "the tormented soul of Spain." *Fabled Shore*, although necessarily referring to ancient invasions and massacres, does not concern itself with the political aspect of contemporary Spain. Connolly saw as a good "omen" the "arrival on the scene of a warm and precise latter-day humanist, coaxing her little car along the hot road with her bathing dress drying on the back and a Roman atlas or two beside her, seeing exactly what her eye registers and implementing it from the information to be obtained in some accurate textbooks, preferring buildings to people and a good beach to most buildings, aroused to ecstasy only by the operation . . . of her excellent historical imagination on the beauty around her . . ." (*Sunday Times*, May 15, 1949, 4).

A travel book may be said, in the last analysis, to travel on its style. The style of *Fabled Shore*, to which Nicolson gives the highest praise, is extremely flexible. The informative details are set down in a clear and businesslike way; that the book is, as Connolly observed, "extremely useful" the present writer can bear out, having used it as a guide, as well as a companion, in driving along the same route (under much less arduous conditions) in 1963. But it is the versatility of the style in the constant motion back and forth between swift glimpses of beauty, ironic observations on a present-day situation or a historical event, defenses of modes of life or of architecture currently underrated, moments of personal delight or of unavoidable discomfort or of impish mischief (when at loggerheads with some stupid regulation), evocations of long-vanished life from the ruined mosaics of a Roman villa–it is this versatility of style that holds the reader fascinated.

In her descriptions, her varying rhythms are as active as the words in recreating the sights and emotions:

I dropped into the green water and swam out; Malaga across the bay was golden pale like a pearl; the little playa of Torremolinos had fishing boats and nets on it and tiny lapping waves. Near me was a boat with fishermen, who were hacking mussels off the rocks and singing. The incredible beauty of the place and hour, of the smooth opal morning sea, shadowing to deep jade beneath the rocks, of the spread of the great bay, of the climbing, winding garden above with the blue shadows on its white walls, the golden pumpkins, the grey-green spears of the aloes, the arcaded terrace and rambling jumble of low buildings was like the returning memory of a dream long forgotten. (138-39)

Nicolson commented on her avoidance of "decorative" polysyllables and her effective use of simple words, often monosyllabic: "Over the ravine great birds flew with wide wings" (141). The living motion of the vegetation contrasts with the firmness of the earth: "little vines scramble over the lower slopes of the great hill flanks" (11).

She defends the baroque against those who find it "absurd," giving in a few words the essence of the mode: "an animated figure in every Corinthian columned and fluted recess; bishops, saints and angels stand with elegant firmness in niches and on pediments, or balance with charming precariousness on curved whorls, all pyramiding up to the arched summit, where, above the Assumption in an apse, voluminously garbed angels support a shield. The evening sunshine blazing on this ornately beautiful scene made it appear the golden gate of some urbane and cheerful paradise" (115).

Part of the charm of the book lies in a mythopoeic element: this traveler is at times a child adventuring among mighty opponents: "My front bumper was jerked off, beginning a long series of such decadences. Throughout the nearly four thousand miles of road that I covered in the peninsula, I learnt that cars are not so firmly held together as one had hoped. One piece after another is liable to drop from them; there is a sudden intimidating clatter . . ." (25). "Decadences" is one of the occasional puns from a favorite scholarly field, etymology. The mythopoeic process may involve the traveler in temporal ambivalences: "It was, I reflected, one of my last Mediterranean bathes, for it was only about twenty-five miles to the Straits, the Pillars of Hercules, where the known world ended and the dark bottomless void of the misty Ocean began. I drove along towards this dubious bourne, the blue of the Middle Sea still bright and familiar at my side" (145).

Historical situations may be sketched in speculative questions: "Did the young Moors of Peñíscola stare and jeer and throw stones from the ramparts as the fallen anti-pope and his cardinals swept in and out of the ancient church, or up and down those steep streets to the little beach and back (but not to bathe, for they condemned that as an infidel and unchristian practice)? Did poor Papa Luna look a proud pope, or merely a lonely, weary, schismatic, disgruntled elderly man? And what was the attitude towards him of the Peñíscola parish priest?" (82-83). Surprising turns are frequent: "The present bishops of Gerona must look back with some wistfulness to the grand feudal state kept by their medieval predecessors, their wealth and wide lands, their trains of slaves and concubines, their noble libraries, their great monasteries (though the abbots often gave them trouble), the dues they extorted from their vassals, even the wars of envy and fear waged against them by the counts of Barcelona and the kings of Aragon . . ." (29).

The effect of formal ritual may be conveyed by a slight shift to an older word order: "This chapel was originally Moorish, and from its tower the One God was for centuries daily declared" (150). She may suddenly force words to carry an unusual weight; after quoting a description by Strabo of New Carthage, she observes: "Yes, New Carthage was a place then" (118). A recourse of style that she frequently uses throughout her writing is the repetition of a trite expression to bring out the irony of our assurance in having taken the matter for granted: when the car would break down, it was necessary to find one's way to a town and "bring back mechanics with the necessary tools. It was not always quite easy to explain to the mechanics what the necessary tools would be" (25).

A winding sentence may go from the sea gate to the top of the rock fortress of Tossa: ". . . through . . . the Torre de las Horas, one enters the Vila Vella, that medieval twist of steep ancient streets and ruinous houses that climbs Monte Gardí to the summit where the ruined shell of a fourteenth-century Gothic church stands, framing with its empty broken arch the view of the little beach below, where the painted fishing boats lie at the sea's edge" (43). Esthetic appreciation need not exclude ironical amusement; delightful incongruities of diction appear in her description of Jerez: ". . . it is full of lovely buildings . . . the rich plateresque façade of the Cabildo Viejo, . . . with its crowded population of scultpured beings–Hercules, scowling gorilla-like with his club, a dominating but anonymous military man, said to be an emperor, the four cardinal virtues (female, intoxicated, and perched precariously on the cornices of the side portals) and a charming frieze of satyrs, vases, garlands and boys" (175-76).

For all the irony, however, there are many passages of romantic appreciation: "I made my bed in the roofless apse of what must have been once a chapel; all night the wind whispered and moaned coldly about the Sacred Cape; the long beams of the lighthouse, and of that of Sagres, speared and shafted the desolate wastes of the sea which bounds the known world" (198). And the final sentence (though made up largely of monosyllables) is highly incantatory: ". . . as through the long bright centuries before the first Tyrian ship swam into Gadir bay, Iberians and Lusitanians sailed and fished and fought and grew the olive and the vine" (198).[3]

When Rose Macaulay finished the book, she must have felt satisfaction in having herself filled a need she had earlier praised E. M. Forster for filling in his book on Alexandria: "One would wish more guides like this, for the imagination and mind are fed, fact and detail are informed by beauty . . . the book is what any tourist wants and too seldom gets" (see ch. V, sec. 6). Connolly found the book falling "on the reader like a bolt from the blue, heavy with the mildest of explosives–accurate information, swift as the fleeting mental processes of the freedom-loving, pleasure-liking and learned lady who made it" (*Sunday Times*, May 15, 1949, 4).

IV   The World My Wilderness

In spite of the resilient spirit shown in her two travel-history books, Rose Macaulay was still profoundly affected by the distressing personal events of 1941-42, and by the whole tragedy of the war. Ruins, which had appeared in her novel of 1930, now took on a symbolism that embraced the wastage of the wars of the past two decades, the accompanying spiritual desolation, and the ineluctable transiency of man and his works. But, as Anthony Burgess has pointed out in discussing this symbol in her writing, "ruins are ambivalent, since they represent a survival as well as a death" (ch. V, n. 5). In 1950 came *The World My Wilderness,* a novel that she described as being "about the ruins of the City [traditional business center of London], and the general wreckage of the world that they seem to stand for. And about a rather lost and strayed and derelict girl who made them her spiritual home" (*L*, 27).

"The World My Wilderness," wrote the *Times Literary Supplement* reviewer in an extended article that looked back over her novels as far as *Potterism,* "contains a deeper note of compassion than any of her earlier novels; not her most amusing book, it is certainly her most moving one" (May 12, 1950, 292). Only the novelist's close friends could know to what extent the predicaments of the characters symbolized aspects of her own anguish at that period. After her death, the publication of the letters that she began writing in August, 1950, to the Anglican priest Father Johnson (ch. I, sec. 5) made these facts clear.[4]

In the novel, the derelict girl, appropriately named Barbary, is an under-sized, under-educated seventeen-year-old whose adolescence has been spent among the junior aids to the Maquis where the foothills of the Pyrenees come down to the Mediterranean at Collioure. Her mother, Helen, had left her husband, an eminent English barrister, in 1939 and had settled in the tiny French port as the mistress, then the wife, of Maurice Michel, a robust, jolly man who had resigned himself to collaborating in matters of economics with the conquerors but not in politics; on the contrary, he had helped several Allied soldiers escape into Spain. But shortly after the Armistice he was found drowned in the bay, a victim of the unpacified, lawless band that included Barbary and his own young son Raoul. Confused loyalties, exacerbated by confused personal emotions in a disrupted society—Barbary, her mother's pet, had been jealous of Maurice—and precocious initiation into violence and torture had given these young people a concept of life as an inferno.

Helen, a large, handsome, free-living woman, the daughter of an Irish lord, physically lazy but mentally keen—her pursuits include Greek, Latin, and Provençal literature, chess, and painting—is not entirely integrated as a fictional character. But, in those traits that come into play in her separate relations with each of the other characters, she constitutes a remarkably effective force. Between her and her daughter lies the unmentionable barrier of Maurice's death. To get the girl away from the chaotic life of the region, and from her own numb daily resentment, Helen sends her back to London, where Sir Gulliver Deniston has taken as his second wife Pamela, a capable, proper, athletic, and unimaginative young woman, a type formed at Roedean. Although Raoul is also going to London, to study with an uncle, Barbary is utterly desolated at being exiled from her mother and her baby stepbrother.

Sir Gulliver—brilliant, ironic, detached (but without the triumphant generosity that accompanied these qualities in Rosamund Ilbert and Rome Garden)—is disappointed to find a daughter gauche and unkempt. He arranges for her to study art, for which she has some talent; but he makes no attempt to resume more than a monitory relation with her. Pamela, jealous of Helen, offers Helen's child no love but only impersonal decencies; and she requires adherence to a rigid social scheme that is meaningless to Barbary. The two young exiles, desperately homesick among the "meaningless grey city streets," discover the vast bombed-out area beyond St. Paul's, the torn ruins and shells of houses, shops, and churches, "a wrecked and flowering wilderness"; "these broken habitations, this stony rubbish, seemed natural to them" (50-52). The waste "had familiarity, as of a place long known; it had the clear, dark logic of a dream; it made a lunatic sense, as the unshattered streets and squares did not; it was the country that one's soul recognized and knew" (61). They spend all their spare time there and keep house in the top of one of the ruins. As they expect, other members of London's "Resistance" resort to this area—youths who had deserted from the army, "spivs" and their girls, who are dodging what Barbary and Raoul regard as the English "Gestapo."

The bitter social comedy played in Sir Gulliver's house intensifies. When Barbary comes in late to a company dinner with dirt

from the ruins on her unchanged dress, her father permits himself
some elegant persiflage: "May one ask what branch of art you
have been practising this evening? Drawing in charcoal?" (60).
Later that evening Pamela comments: "You do behave in the
oddest way, I must say. I mean, I know you grew up abroad, and
all that . . ." (62).

In August, Barbary is to go with them to her uncle's shooting
lodge on the Scottish moors, a region she would love were it not
for the "intimidating family of sons and daughters, . . . all jolly,
handsome, modishly dressed, and formidably efficient at catching
and killing Highland animals." Pamela "seemed to have clothes
for all emergencies and occupations that might, in the Highlands,
arrive; a suit for catching salmon and trout, a suit for catching
grouse, a suit for peering through telescopes at stags, a suit for
playing golf . . . ." With unconscious irony, Pamela asks her step-
daughter, "I don't suppose you shoot, do you?" Barbary's response
is unvoiced: "I don't suppose . . . *you've* ever sniped at Gestapo
in forests. I bet you've no Gestapo suit." On being told that one
of these cousins captains "the eleven," Barbary asks, "Eleven
what?" Pamela reacts with some sharpness: "You might pretend
to know just a little about things, like other people" (81-83).

At Arshaig, Barbary assimilates her inquisitive psychiatrist
uncle to the Gestapo; and, fearing the confessions she knows he
can force her to make, she steals some money from her aunt's
drawer and escapes back to London. Spending her days at the
ruins, she paints postcard sketches, which sell well to tourists.
But frequently she is overwhelmed by her alienation and by the
guilt of not having made the extreme effort that might have prevented the murder of Maurice. In the ruined church next door to
her ruined eyrie, she paints scenes of hell and acts out religious
rituals to meet her desperate need.

Eventually, when making a try at shoplifting, Barbary and
Raoul are caught by the police; and, in using a Maquis trick to
help Raoul escape, she falls into a cellar and is badly hurt. Helen
rushes back to London, the adults assess their various degrees of
guilt, and the mother takes her daughter to be with her–away
from both London and the Collioure Maquis–in Paris. (Helen
reveals to Sir Gulliver that the girl's real father was a Spanish

painter.) Barbary, too, has learned; what Helen tells her, she had already come to realize:

> You and your friends thought Maurice was a *collaborateur,* didn't you. What a stupid word that is. He never betrayed anyone; all he did was to make the best of things and live in the world as it was, on terms with everyone round him, German and French [a way of life urged by the clergy of the region]. You all felt this was betrayal; perhaps it was; and God knows what else you thought he had done. So Maurice, who was so kind and would never hurt anyone. . . . Well, that's over now. Except that I shall always miss him, and that Roly will grow up without a father. (231-32)

Barbary has also learned that she must be generous enough to share her mother's affection with the man or men whom Helen will need, through the years, as lovers.

Barbary's desperation and Helen's torpor are not the only reactions to the war that are presented. Another child of Helen's is Richie, who fought in the war, was captured, escaped, and is now studying at Cambridge. Frank Swinnerton, in his review, spoke of the "charming sketches of character (best of all, in my opinion, Barbary's undergraduate brother, who is perfect)" (*Spectator,* CLXXXIV, [May 12, 1950], 653). Richie's reaction from his "unbelievable years . . . of barbarism" is "towards gentleness, towards bland tolerance, towards an excessive civility." In his nostalgic pursuit of aristocratic culture, "he was impelled sometimes beyond his reasoning self, to grasp at the rich, trailing panoplies, the swinging censers, of churches from whose creeds and uses he was alien, because at least they embodied some continuance, some tradition . . ." During "all this frightening evanescence and dissolution the historic churches kept their strange courses, kept their improbable, incommunicable secret, linking the dim past with the disrupted present and intimidating future, frail, tough chain of legend, myth, and mystery, stronghold of reaction and preserved values" (149-50). Less than a year after the publication of this novel, Rose Macaulay had made a formal confession to an Anglican priest and had resumed regular worship in the Church in which so many of her ancestors had been clergymen (*L,* 57; see also 50, and *LL,* 18).

In *The World My Wilderness* the City ruins are assimilated, in some memorable pasages, to the ruins of many earlier civilizations: "Among the hidden Companies' Halls, deep below where guildmen had for centuries feasted and conferred, among the medieval bases and only a few feet now above the Roman stones, . . . the wild cats scream, the new traders, the pirates, the racketeers, the black marketeers, the robber bands, roam and lurk." Or, in a more homely vein, "The little squares and courts . . . were quite gone" and "the great buildings that had replaced [them] . . . ; the crickets in the brambly copse that sprawled where Windsor Court and Wood Street Square had been, chirped like the ghosts of a chatter of burned typewriters" (182-83). Three years after the novel, the author published a compendious book, *Pleasure of Ruins,* at which she was already at work.

V Pleasure of Ruins

The wartime ruins in London had not, of course, been the first ruins to which Rose Macaulay had given an important part in a novel. There were those extensive Mayan ruins, overlaid by a ruined Spanish monastery, in *Staying with Relations* (1930). Her "ruins-passion" (*LL*, 142) kept her hard at work for several years through a series of minor though debilitating illnesses, researching on ruins of all times and places, and, more especially, on what human emotions had been aroused by the spectacle of these ruins, until in the summer of 1953, at the age of seventy-two, she was able to gratify her publisher with the completed text and the collected period illustrations of *Pleasure of Ruins.* Appropriately, while she was correcting the proofs of this lengthy work, a fire devastated the sitting-room of her apartment; but she was able to see the book into print before Christmas.[5]

Pleasure of Ruins is very different from *Fabled Shore;* for, while it suggests to travelers places to go and enhances their enjoyment, it is in no sense a guidebook. In fact, since it is ordered in part by the moods of different periods and in part by categories of buildings, its focus is continually being shifted geographically and chronologically. Instead of recreating that feeling that accounts for much of the charm of *Fabled Shore*–of the narrator being physically at a specific spot–this book is concerned with giving the "ruin-sentiments," "ruin-discourses," "Ruinenlust," "Ruinensehnsucht," "Ruinenempfindsamkeit" of other "ruino-logers."

The author's objectivity was praised by the *New Statesman* reviewer: "She must have seen a fabulous number of ruins with her own eyes but is far too skillful a writer to betray exactly when she is with us in person and when she has slipped us over for the moment to some other conductor" (John Summerson, XLVI [December 12, 1953] 764). These other conductors may have expressed their ruin-sentiments in Greek, Latin, or any of several modern languages. As the reviewer in the *Observer* noted, "Miss Macaulay's reading, above all her hunt for illustrations, must have been great, but the book wears its burden of scholarship very lightly." Part of the lightness consists in doing the reader the courtesy of assuming that, if he is interested in travel and history, he will be able to read along with the compiler in the modern languages and in the easier passages of Latin. The reviewer continued: "Miss Macaulay's style is simple, direct and–unlike that of some of her more excitable travellers–almost unjewelled. It is her thoughts that are dark, rich, surprising and romantic" (R. Furneaux Jordan, December 6, 1953, 9).

The book opens with an offering of biblical passages of "ruin-triumph," and the author comments: "One cannot distinguish too nicely, or too sharply define the separation of aesthetic pleasure from vindictive. In what proportions, for instance, were the elements mixed in the magnificent poetic ruin pictures painted in windy words by the Hebrew poets . . ?" (1). In the eighteenth-century vogue for building artificial ruins, what was the proportion between esthetic pleasure and "the general Weltschmerz, Sehnsucht, malaise, nostalgia, Angst, frustration, sickness, passion of the human soul" of which ruin "is the eternal symbol" (23)?

The long section of "The Stupendous Past" presents Middle Eastern, Greek, and Roman ruins, distinguishing those that by their nature, or that of their surroundings, have become unidentifiable mounds; those that have been relentlessly quarried away; those that have sunk into a marsh or a sea (perhaps to remain visible at low tide); and those that have been pushed into the earth under the weight of several later cities. The sight of the excavated bulls of Nimrud, of the honey-colored standing or prone columns of Palmyra, of the broken Colosseum have produced a whole gamut of emotions, varying with the period, personality, and purpose of the viewer–and she quotes ancient conquerors, voyaging clergymen, antiquaries, romantic travelers, archaeologists, poets. But all who have seen these great works have experienced "a soaring of the imagination into the high empyrean where huge episodes are tangled with myths and dreams . . ." (40). The section "Ghostly Streets" includes the two cities buried by Vesuvius: "To that fortunate disturbance . . . we owe an infinity of pleasure. . . . Contemporaries of the catastrophe deplored it with horrified fascination" (286-87). As for the courtiers of Naples who began the excavations, the author cannot forgive their "stupidity, clumsiness and greed," which scattered and destroyed so much from the unique cache (291). In one section she discusses the complicated question of restoration: What human uses does it serve? Do ruins of certain periods and in certain climates suffer, or gain, more from restoration than others? Why? How should specific British ruins be treated? How do people of this decade feel about the ruins from World War II?

And so, with every kind of consideration, the book presents its topic. As Raymond Mortimer observed in his review, it "is better suited to the bedside than to a quick perusal. . . . The quotations she offers are themselves a delicious anthology . . ." (*Sunday Times*, December 6, 1953, 5). Her own passages range from irony through comic appreciation–"The eleven years of Mr Wood's toil were to him passionately exciting; stinted of money by the British Museum, frustrated by Pashas and Beys and Turkish workmen, robbed by burglars, stabbed by local maniacs, haunted by brigands, injured by falls, prostrated by sickness, visited by tourists who only cared for their food and ignored his ruins, and by others who picked up and pocketed valuable fragments, he indomitably kept at it . . ." (322)–to a musing regret for such a lost city as that hedonistic Sybaris, which "lies, wrecked and drowned, but safe from quarrying, protected these thousands of years by river mud and earth . . .; its fallen columns lying lovely and intact. . . . A complete civilization lies beneath our feet as we tread the marshy ground through which the Cratis winds" (214-15). Her versatile style triumphs once more in such passages.

The book is long, but much material that the author had prepared had to be omitted; and some passages suffer from the attempt to cover too much–in these the thought seems to race along without taking time for her usual surprises in turns of thought and in diction. Some of the best writing, with imaginative descriptions and the trying out of ideas, comes in the two final pages, on the "new ruins" from the war.

VI   Towers of Trebizond

Pleasure of Ruins had come out on December 7, 1953, and by February, 1954, Rose Macaulay was busy making corrections for the second edition and reviewing C.E.M. Joad's *Folly Farm* for the *Times Literary Supplement*. In March she wrote Father Johnson: "I am reviewing too many books; they take my time" (*LL*, 147). The publishers of *Ruins* wanted to send her on a trip that she could write about, while the publishers of her novels were urging her to do another novel. A novel was Father Johnson's preference and, after a little thought, hers too. Soon she was organizing her ideas for it. She spent the month of June on a trip –a trip was involved after all–that included the Mediterranean coast of Turkey and the Black Sea coast as far east as Trebizond (Trabzon).

This trip complemented the one to the Near East the preceding year, when *Ruins* was almost finished. Much of her time continued to be taken up by reviewing and by participation in B.B.C. radio discussion programs. Late in 1955 she wrote Father Johnson: "I am still struggling to finish the novel: shortage of time is acute, and will wreck my life and all my undertakings. I should like to have time for geology and cosmology–perhaps one day I shall. Why *do* we pray that '[the dead] may have rest?' Rest is *not* what we shall want, surely, but more scope for work and new knowledge" (*LL*, 212). In September, 1956, *The Towers of Trebizond* was published, a month after her seventy-fifth birthday. It was awarded the James Black Tait prize.

The Towers of Trebizond is an extraordinary work; John Betjeman, the Anglican critic, hailed it as "the best book she has written, and that is saying a lot" (*Daily Telegraph*, September 14, 1956, 8). Almost all the other reviewers gave it high praise; when it was published in the United States the following spring, it became a "best-seller" (Rose Macaulay herself felt that it belonged to a class of intellectual "minority" novels that are "forced into best-sellers by good reviews, but would never be naturally so" [*LL*, 255]). In spite of the almost universal delight in the book, the critics by no means agreed as to its main theme or mood. The book is indeed a teaser for criticism, for any unimaginative application of criteria of genres would condemn it to be judged very faulty.

Orville Prescott, reviewing it in the *New York Times*, found it

an utter delight, the most brilliantly witty and captivatingly charming book I have read since I can't remember when. Probably too odd and surprising to be anything but caviar to the general, the book seems certain to be welcomed with joy by many discriminating readers who will be tempted to use it as a touchstone with which to judge the literary taste of others. . . . To enjoy and understand this glittering tour de force it is necessary to realize that it is not a novel. It is a book about travel in Turkey, a collection of miniature essays and a comic satire of modern life disguised as a novel. (April 10, 1957, 31)

Harold Hobson of the *Christian Science Monitor* found it "urbane and accomplished, . . . eloquent, poetic, witty, high-handed, serious and sad" (October 11, 1956, 10). Walter Havighurst continued this line of thought:

Here is a blend of pagan and Christian, of the Church and the world, a blend which the novel uses with steadily increasing richness. It is a discursive book, crowded with pictures and alive with observations. . . . Outwardly "The Towers of Trebizond" is a zestful, irreverent pilgrimage through cruel and haunted lands. It moves easily between the fables of antiquity and a modern instance of illicit love—love which in this book is not an act but an idea and which achieves an interest unknown to the undress writers. And here the novel turns inward to a search for what the Church can offer; the journey to Trebizond and Jerusalem parallels an agnostic's search for grace. Only a writer of extraordinary wit, learning, and skill could treat this theme with a lightness which does not diminish its gravity. (*Saturday Review*, XL [April 13, 1957], 15, 48).

The author was distressed that some readers missed the "gravity" completely and saw the book as merely a satire on the Church and its clergy. She wrote her sister that she had meant the book "to be about the struggle of good and evil, its eternal importance, and the power of the Christian Church over the soul, to torment and convert" (S, 281, 199).

The external action is a picaresque sequence of incidents that ramble toward a tragic climax. The chief character is Laurie, an unmarried person under forty, who is adulterously in love with Vere; but which lover is of which sex is not made explicit until the last pages—after the death of Vere—and the author hoped the reviewers would not inform the readers,[6] for ". . . so much of life is common to both sexes" (LL, 232). The ambiguity, real at first, becomes a game of virtuosity later when the reader has rightly guessed that, although Laurie is very adequately human, Laurie is not masculine enough to be a man.

As an aide, Laurie accompanies her High Church aunt Dot (a dottier version of Dr. Kate Marlowe) and very High Church Father Hugh Chantry-Pigg on a trip to Turkey to explore the possibilities of setting up Church of England missions there. They take along a jeep and aunt Dot's white camel—" 'Take my camel, dear,' said my aunt Dot, as she climbed down from this animal on her return from High Mass" has found a place among the famous opening sentences in literature. The theme of sin is soon made explicit when Father Chantry-Pigg rebukes Laurie sharply and bids her return to a state of grace; but she feels this would "break my life to bits" (72).

East of Trebizond aunt Dot and the priest fulfill their—or at least aunt Dot's—dream (thwarted by mid-century passport rigidities) of exploring Russia by crossing the mountainous frontier and pretending to seek political asylum. After their disappearance, Laurie, whose conscience enjoys an uneasy slumber, makes her way, partly by camel and partly in the comfortable car of a friend whose plagiarism she has accidentally discovered, to Alexandretta (Iskenderon), where Vere has asked her to meet him when the yachting party of the press lord (Potterism) whom he is accompanying calls there. After this delightful but brief rendezvous, she rides the camel through Syria and Jordan to Jerusalem and to antique sites in Israel. Then she returns to Oxfordshire, bringing the camel and a small ape, to which she proposes to try to impart a moral sense in an experiment that will parallel at greater speed the slow process of human evolution. A few months later aunt Dot and Father Chantry-Pigg escape safely from Russia. Laurie and Vere drive to Venice for a gay, love-filled holiday; as they re-enter London in the Sunday evening traffic, Laurie, at the wheel, in a burst of euphoric foolhardiness asserts her right against an usurping bus; and Vere is instantly killed. On this "slender story" is constructed the "narrative full of splendor" (Havighurst).

The "splendor" is a mosaic of which the pieces (colored variously with satire, restrained lyricism, symbolism, intellectual musing)—scattered and continually reappearing—are travel description and comment, speculation on many aspects of religion and on the potentialities of human nature, and confession. Glinting out from these are tangential ideas and much sheer fun.

What holds these elements together? If the action is loose, it continually affords occasions for one or another—or several—of the themes; and these themes are symbolically related. But the most important continuum is one of the aspects of the confession: the voice of the first-person narrator.[7] Actually, it is a double voice—perhaps not intended to be so as a formal element, but, since the writer was not primarily a formalist, permitted for the sake of the richness that results. The moral frame of the book is Laurie's fictional confession and, doubling it, the confessional testimony of the writer. As Frye has pointed out, "Nearly always some theoretical and intellectual interest in religion, politics, or art plays a leading role in the confession," and here it is the speaker's relation to religion.[8] The narration is done ostensibly by Laurie, but a voice is frequently heard through hers—that of the experienced elderly woman who looks back at her own Laurie aspect and at her life as a whole. A rich voice, it is not limited to the expression of moral probings but conveys the witty, teasing, erudite thoughts of the author of the whole sequence of Macaulay writings.

Laurie is akin to those varied non-conforming girls and young women from Betty Crevequer, in the 1907 novel, through Denham Dobie and Meg Yarde; but she is unmistakably different from any one of them—older and more experienced, better read (although much less erudite than her creator), of adequate worldly know-how, somewhat weary with a mid-century defeatism; but she is graced, at the same time, with a certain childlike accept-ance like that of Lucy Hope, another form of which is mid-century ironic optimism. The author wrote Father Johnson: "I adopted for Laurie a rather goofy, rambling prose style, to put the story at one remove from myself. I find that many readers and reviewers like this style, and some say they have caught it" (*LL*, 232).

The *New Yorker* reviewer found that "it is . . . the author's prose that keeps one going . . . ." (XXXIII [June 1, 1957], 117). The reviewer for the *Reporter* questioned, however, the wisdom of using this style: ". . . if, in the interests of dead-pan humor, one connects with the simple conjunctive 'and' such subject matter as theology and piscatology and adultery and Byzantium and Billy Graham, the effect is to dissolve everything in the same stream of reverie" (XVI [June 13, 1957], 47). Occasional passages justify this complaint–those that betray a willed elfishness. But, in gen-eral, this style is surely intended to demonstrate that Laurie's refusal of the meaningful life offered in religion has reduced her to a state where values are becoming hopelessly confused.

In this far from simple novel, this style also skeptically ques-tions these values. "From time to time," Laurie says, "I knew what I had lost. But nearly all the time, God was a bad second . . ." (72). And "I was getting into a stage when I was not quite sure what sin was" (159). Laurie feels her estrangement from the Church of her ancestors as a tragedy, but she cannot return to it without impoverishing her life of good things of this world which, as a human being as well as (and if) an immortal soul, she must greatly cherish. As believer, she finds the right choice too hard; as skeptic, she finds the right choice uncertain. The human condition as tragedy is basic to the book and, in the last pages, is acutely presented; but the human condition as comedy is more exten-sively explored.

The motif of the reduction of values is introduced on the first page: ". . . this car"–aunt Dot's Morris–"had been stolen from her by some Anglican bishop from outside the Athenaeum annexe while she was dining there one evening with Professor Gilbert Murray and Archbishop David Mathew" (9).[9] One of the con-tinuing jokes is that "they are all writing their Turkey books"–and several actual writers on location are encountered or at least named (21). In one of its aspects, this is Rose Macaulay's Turkey book: "If it were nothing else, Miss Macaulay's latest novel would be a superb travel book" (Hobson). Like *Fabled Shore,* it gives the sense of a particular human being coping with inns, roads, local customs, immigration officials, difficult weather, and the urges of her own temperament. Also, as in the earlier book, actuality merges with myth: after a few days of traveling alone, Laurie finds her funds running short; enviously she peruses her phrase book, whose hero, "a very greedy man, would order, one after the other, young marrows stuffed with minced mutton and herbs," etc., etc., "washing it down with exotic wines," while "I had to do with bread, cheese, soup, yoghourt, and an occasional egg" (167-68).

In a passage that satirizes the B.B.C.'s banal distortion of native scenes–and readers up on their Siegfried Sassoon will enjoy the fact that into whatever folkloric town their recording van goes "everybody suddenly bursts out singing" (22)–the voices of Laurie and her creator are both heard. Round the recording van "stood a crowd of Trapezuntines staring"; the interpreter was asked to inquire "what the favourite games in Trabzon were, and how much football was played, and was it rugger or soccer, but the answer, said the interpreter, was tric-trac, so the second half of the question did not arise." Aunt Dot, the feminist, "asked in Turkish, 'What do the girls play?' but did not stop for the answer"; for she knew that they never got a chance to play. In "Trapezuntines" is recognized the author's fascination with such words; and the satire on British games recalls her many comments on this subject–recalling them is part of the fun; in the Bacon allusion, her fine hand appears; but the overall style is Laurie's. Occasionally the voice is entirely the author's: "The real Trebizond . . . was . . . in the disused wrecked Byzantine churches that brooded, forlorn, lovely, ravished and apostate ghosts, about the hills and shores of that lost empire" (80).

In this book, as in *The World My Wilderness,* the places are felt to have a dramatic relation to the travelers. The adventures of the *Argo* along these shores are a symbol of primitive passions; those readers who are up on their Byron will enjoy Laurie's recognition of the harms that passion entails: "I remembered how

Euripides had made Medea's nurse complain, 'Oh how I wish that an embargo/ Had kept in port the good ship Argo . . .'" (181). The serio-comic drive down to Troy evokes in these classically educated travelers a nostalgia for the departed mythical grandeur of the place. It serves to define the characters, by their individual interpretations and enthusiasms, and by their sympathetic or jealous reactions to the views of competing writers.

That the visible ruins of Troy are disappointing to their dreams contributes to the religious theme; like Laurie's indefinitely postponed repentance, the walls that the guide identified as being of Priam's palace were actually "too little and too late" (35). Laurie is tormented by nostalgia for the beloved ceremonies of the Church; and readers up on their Hebrew alphabet will enjoy her thought that the dark, sad inhabitants standing about the road near Troy looked "like those obscure, dejected, maladjusted and calamity-prone characters who come into Tenebrae, such as Aleph, Teth, Beth, Calph, Jod, Ghimel, Mem, and the rest" (40). Religion and man's use of it is one of the meanings of such a travel passage as: "I went to Nazareth, which was full of tourists and touting guides and fake holy places, and I went on to the Sea of Galilee, and this was so beautiful that I stayed by it for several days, . . . going with the fishermen in their boats while they cast their nets, fishing alone from the shore . . ." (213).

Earlier, when Laurie is returning to Trebizond alone, she feels that the place has "some strange hidden meaning, which I must try to dig up" (142). She spends some time every day in the ruined citadel and palace, envisioning the splendor of the Byzantine civilization. Trebizond has several meanings in the book, but one of them is an allegorical representation of the Church. In a letter to Father Johnson, the author tells him: "Trebizond stands for not merely the actual city (tho' this comes in and a lovely place it is) but for the ideal and romantic and nostalgic vision of the Church which haunts the person who narrates the story" (*LL*, 219). Like Trebizond, the last city of the Byzantine Empire to fall, the Christian Church seems (in the voice of the elder narrator) "like a great empire on its way out, that holds its subjects by poetic force, its fantastic beauty heightened by insecurity . . . ." Yet, "though forever reeling, the towers do not fall . . ." (244; see Burgess, ch. V, n. 5).

In a discussion with an agnostic friend Laurie grants that the historical aspect of the Church–its strange origin, its disputes and cruelty, its curious developments–is "odd"; but she also insists that this aspect is "mostly irrelevant to what matters," which is "the light of the spirit." She has a vision of "the Trebizond of the world's dreams, of my own dreams, . . . luminously enspelled in the most fantastic unreality, yet the only reality . . . standing beyond my reach yet I had to be inside . . ." (209-10). The vision appears also in the epigraph, composed by the author: "Those who have once desired it cannot let it go . . . ." There is later in the book a long passage, partly in dialogue, that amounts to an essay on Rose Macaulay's views of the Christian Church after a long life of thinking about it. She agrees with its critics that many points of doctrine are ill-founded, that "theology seems the only science which does not keep adapting its views and its manuals to new knowledge as it turns up," that "nothing in the world . . . could be as true" as each church thinks its teachings are (236-38).

In a letter to her sister shortly before her death, she wrote that ". . . religious belief is too uncertain and shifting a ground (with me) to speak of lying or truth in connection with it. One believes in patches, and it is a vague, inaccurate word. I could never say 'I believe in God' in the same sense that I could say 'I believe in the sun & moon & stars' " (S, 282). Always averse to bigotry in religion, during her last years she "made a point of taking part in the worship of various Nonconformist churches" (S, 23); and, in the same month in which the book was published, she said, "I have started a new group, called Inter-communionists . . ." (S, 236). In the novel Father Hugh withholds himself from ecumenicism, and even kindly aunt Dot, when she declares that "dissenters are often excellent Christian people," adds, "though . . . you must always remember that *we* are *right*" (16). Laurie, like her creator, sees virtue in what many people condemn in the Anglican Church, the latitude in the form of service that is permitted: ". . . our Church is very wonderful and comprehensive, and . . . this variety that it has is one of its glories" (54).

Though aunt Dot is a zealous High Church woman, her mission is motivated even more by her feminism; and she sets forth triumphantly, in blue linen slacks, holding scarlet reins, on the white camel–white plumes waving from its head–to help Turkish women toward sexual equality by converting the Moslems to the Church of England. In a chapter on Rose Macaulay in *The Ark of God,* Douglas Stewart comments: ". . . like the gargoyles on a medieval cathedral, the camel too is contributing to the splendour of the whole . . . " (London, 1961, p. 101). But secretly she is motivated most by love of travel; her catechism, like Laurie's, would hold that "travel is the chief end of life" (13).

When Laurie gets to Jerusalem, she unexpectedly runs into her mother, a sort of upper-class Mrs. Arthur (ch. IV, sec. 9). When they drive out to Bethlehem, a charming fantasy results:

> Whenever my mother was in Bethlehem she got some of these jackets or tunics. . . . She had a notion that all the New Testament women had shopped there, and that on the Sabbath they had all put on these velvet coats, and walked out in them, and she pictured all the Marys, that is, the Blessed Virgin, and Mary of Bethany, and Mary Cleophas, and Mary Magdalene (so unjustly defamed by posterity on no evidence), as well as Martha, and old Anna, and the woman taken in adultery, and the woman with the ointment who was a sinner, and all the other women, walking out in these black velvet coats embroidered with gold thread, and over their heads they wore shawls of black handmade lace. (204)

As in any work of sophisticated wit, there are some passages that amount to semi-private jokes between the author and one or another limited group of readers–travelogue readers, Anglicans, London Anglicans, or readers of certain Sunday papers. In no instance, however, need the reader be a member of any special "in"-group to perceive what the general point is; there is nothing "snob" involved; and a certain degree of exciting urgency in regard to the general matters discussed is engendered by these links with actuality. In this category may be listed tangential bits that old Macaulay hands are intended to recognize; the skill with which the author brings them in amounts to a game.

Because of her age when writing this book and because of uncertain health, Rose Macaulay realized that it might well be her last one. She wrote to her sister in March, 1955: "I have an intuition that I shall die in three years, i.e. in 1958, so must bustle about and do a lot of things in the time" (S, 174). Into this type of book, where the action takes place at the level of thought, she could pack even more of her current ideas than into a work of more traditional form. Newspapers and governments come in for satire, especially in connection with aunt Dot's and Father Hugh's Russian interlude. Although this adventure is the least integrated part of the plot, it was highly topical in the mid-1950's when two British physicists had just deserted to Russia and when all countries were jittery from spy-scares and were tightening their visa restrictions. The topic of human cruelty throughout history, and the part in this shared by the Church that deplores the crucifixion of its founder, is brought in when Laurie visits Jerusalem. In that city, too, Laurie defends the "glitter" of the Armenian chapel: "it's like an Aladdin's cave"; she likes churches "either flashy or nobly austere" (207-8)—a protest against spiritual mediocrity that recalls *The Lee Shore*. Linguistics has its turn: Father Hugh, aristocratic and old-fashioned, when moved to speak of howling deserts, "pronounced it hooling, and I believe this is right, like Cowley and owl" (112). With "the Novel of today" being spoken of so much, the young Turkish intellectuals ask Laurie her opinion of "the Poem of today" (65).

The love between Laurie and Vere is seen only at a distance or in retrospect; as described, it is indeed a foeman worthy of the virtuous soul's steel: "And out of this meanness and this selfishness and this lying flow love and joy and peace, beyond anything that can be imagined" (226). And "when we were together, peace flowed about us like music, and fun sprang up between us like a shining fountain" (279). At the close of the book, immediately after Vere's death, Laurie feels that she has lost the meaning of her life and that to return to the Church would be to deny Vere; yet she must always long for that luminous "city." Rose Macaulay wrote to Father Johnson: "I too, you know, felt Laurie's half-stunned insensibility, and even aversion, towards the Church, for some time after the man I had loved for so long died." Laurie, she indicated, would eventually resume her communion (*LL*, 233). In the months after the book was published, the author received many letters from persons who had been moved by it. That the story was related to her own life was then known only to her close friends; to herself, the book must have seemed a memorial offering—half-concealed, half-disclosed.

The central conflict in the book is treated in a manner much more lyric than dramatic; Laurie feels nostalgia for the City of God, but she is not depicted as struggling against her love. The self-regarding, or purely "religious," aspect of her sin is frequently presented; but its effect on Vere's wife, the ethical aspect, is given only brief mention and then after Vere's death. Perhaps this relative unconcern is indicative of the decay of Laurie's conscience. But aside from her relation with Vere, Laurie's sinfulness is mild enough; at most, she is rather indolent and purposeless. The culminating accident–Laurie is legally in the right–is caused by a failure of her usual practical good sense, by a certain willfulness, and by irresponsibility in having taken a "euphoria pill"; Vere's death seems to be interpreted as the one time when Laurie didn't "get by."

Sinfulness, as an element in the book, is dispersed among all the central characters, and it ranges from the spiritual pride of aunt Dot and Father Hugh through the declinations of those jealous, untruthful, and selfish young men Charles and David, to David's outright plagiarism. David's appropriation of Charles' writings after Charles' death indicates a laxity toward which Laurie may be sliding; the "blackmail" that she practices on this erring young man is presented, however, in a comic ambiance and she is fulfilling the social code of not tattling. The scene in which she lets David see how much she knows is the funniest of all the dramatized scenes in the book; the comic style is tantamount to a pardon for her complicity.

Of the non-dramatized passages, the first page, which is packed with wit, and the introductory pages on the mystical affinity between Anglican clergymen and angling are among many that are as entertaining as any that Rose Macaulay had ever written.

CHAPTER 7

An Assessment

THE characteristics that distinguish Rose Macaulay's writing –stylistic mastery, a lively inventiveness, perceptiveness, erudition, and saneness–wear well and would seem to promise a succession of grateful readers. Many of her works have been republished, some several times; and republication has been continuing since her death. During her fifty years of writing, she became, to intellectual readers, something of an institution. Before World War I, her fiction was noted for both sensitivity and wit. In the decade following the war, her extreme avoidance of sentimentality gave the satirical aspect of her work major prominence. But if, as once critic noted, "she had a crisp intolerance of shams and sillinesses,"[1] her derision was far from being ill-humored; and clearly present under her amusing observations was her continuing sense of the tragic nature of life. The historical novel that she wrote early in the 1930's and her last three novels are more explicitly concerned with basic dilemmas in man's condition: "the truth about mankind may be called, if we like, a nightmare shot with light . . . ."[2]

In her fiction there is much praise of "detachment"–of remaining aloof from the probably pointless heat and battle and of stoically contenting oneself with "ironic" observation that sees life as "amusing." Rose Macaulay undoubtedly found much of the heat and battle ill-judged, in regard to both matter and means; but with means of an urbane sort–intelligence and wit–she seldom ceased from mental fight against what she called "the three black jungle horrors": "ignorance, vulgarity, and cruelty" (see ch. V. sec. 7). Ignorance besets all levels of mankind; but, as one of a class who have been fortunate in endowment and training, she tried to see clearly and to guide others to make an effort to do so.

Fiction gave her more scope for the play of her varied powers than did poetry or journalism. Early in her career she evolved a type of fiction that freely makes use of other resources than those of the "novel" in its narrowest definition. Her fiction deals primarily with ideas, preferences, and attitudes rather than with actions, decisions, and emotions; the characters are almost always of the social class traditionally most concerned with the play of ideas—her own. If Northrop Frye's terms are employed, she drew upon the Menippean satire or "anatomy" (ch. II, n. 9) for the device of a crew of characters who, although in the main realistic, could yet be seen to represent a selection of human follies and stupidities—or merely quirks. Her characters are a combination of authentic representation and the imaginative projection of some human potentiality. The situation at the opening of her books is often mildly fey—another aspect of the Menippean satire. She gathered her persons together for a confrontation of ideas—a "Menippean *cena*"—and through this device her irony worked in what a recent critic called "her mocking, generous, exuberant approach" to human follies (Pryce-Jones, 7 [see Bibliography]).

Fascinated by language, Rose Macaulay used it with extraordinary versatility: she moved at ease from eighteenth-century elegance ("wit flatters the reader into borrowed discernment") to Edwardian, Georgian, and mid-century colloquialism ("What I mean is, he kind of likes me—"). Etymology was one of her favorite pursuits. For a time, in the 1930's, she overindulged her taste for donnish preciosity; but, as World War II approached, she abandoned this style. Her skill with rhythms, one of the chief elements of charm in her poems, is a constant delight in her prose, whether she is placing the key-words in an epigram, leading a sinuous discussion through surprising turns, or making a simple statement in monosyllables. Her effects are produced economically: "Few writers, since Jane Austen, have achieved so compact a treatment of English."[3]

In all of Rose Macaulay's work the presence of the "implied author" is strongly felt. In fiction she follows Jane Austen and George Eliot in this respect. "The real pleasure of Rose Macaulay's novels," wrote one critic, "lies principally in the personality of their writer. . . . throughout her novels, we are conscious of a brisk and entertaining companion, who at intervals talks to us herself" (ch. II, n. 3).

[166]

It may be predicted that *They Were Defeated* will long continue to delight students of the seventeenth century; and *They Went to Portugal, Fabled Shore,* and *Pleasure of Ruins* will please readers for whom travel is a complex quest. *The Towers of Trebizond,* with its double voice of immediate and aeonic comment, its complex attitudes, the importance of its frames of reference, its erudition, brilliant wit, and stylistic skill can hardly be soon forgotten. Anthropologically, it seems likely to stand unrivaled for a long time as a gerontological monument.

Orphan Island should continue to be read for its comic interpretation of cultural patterns and for its inventiveness and economic wit; *Crewe Train* for its sensitivity, its fun, and its satiric picture of a literary scene; *Going Abroad* for its erudite fun and its complex sensitive criticism of an important semi-religious movement. In *The World My Wilderness* the depiction of the ruins and of their meaning to the war-confused child is among the memorable presentations of World War II. *The Making of a Bigot, Non-Combatants,* and *Potterism* constitute valuable commentaries on their respective periods by an involved contemporary. *Told by an Idiot,* less immediate in concept, gives with remarkable detail the scroll-like unrolling of nearly half a century of history. All of these delight with their varying proportions of sensitive perception and ironic observation.

In an essay in 1935 Rose Macaulay professed lack of skill with characters, and even lack of interest in them ("Writing," *Personal Pleasures*). Mere transcription apparently failed to challenge her, although a critic of one of her earliest novels testified that, "among her many gifts, [she] possesses that of literary impersonation to a rare degree" (review of *Views and Vagabonds, Spectator,* CVIII [March 2, 1912], 354). But her "created" characters testify to a zestful imagination: Laurie, Father Hugh, aunt Dot, Barbary, Ramón, Dr. Kate, Hero, Denham, Rosamond, Miss Smith, old Jean, Dr. O'Malley, Rome, Leila Yorke, Eddy–down the line, they are memorable; and in the earlier fiction, there are also Benjie in his ironic situation, delightful Peter Margerison, the Crevequer siblings, and that first heroine Rosamund Ilbert with her complex adequacy. The novel reader who misses these creations is the loser.

In Rose Macaulay's writing from the 1920's on, allusion–a conjuring up of the body of mankind's experience–became one of her chief imaginative resources. It can involve a brief phrase or an elaborate network; it is never used to exclude readers–the meaning of the passage is always clear whether the added significance is recognized or not; but, for those who share some phase of her special cultural pattern, the passage is enriched.

Several of her poems would seem equal in interest to the majority of the better poems of the "Georgians." They are sturdy, sensitive, and surprising. *The Secret River*, though a dead end, ranks well with the mood-pieces of the period.

Although "studies" are continually superseded as new critical approaches develop and new facts are turned up, the little *Milton* still seems just and makes lively reading. Nothing in the Forster study has been refuted; although studies of other kinds are rightly complementing it, her "appreciative" treatment of this author, with its witty and good-humored–but alert–discussion of his inadequacies and faults, seems an excellent one as far as it goes. Journalistic essays are fugitive, but many of hers set forth ideas that are still provocative–"she disliked things to be finally settled" (Alan Pryce-Jones in *Encounter* [see ch. V, n. 6])–and might well be collected.

Distinguished though Rose Macaulay's writing is, there is truth in the judgment of one of her life-long admirers: "Her very great natural gifts . . . would seem to have fitted her for greater deeds than any she has performed" (ch. VII, n. 1). Like most writers, she could have pruned to advantage. She sometimes diluted her work with irrelevancies and occasionally introduced bits of over-facile comedy. A tone of archness sometimes appears at what seems an ill-chosen moment. Probably, however, a basic difficulty was that she belonged to a class of gifted amateurs of living who expressed themselves in commentary. She enjoyed using language and found amusement in forming it into novels and essays, but she was more concerned with the presentation of thoughts and with the play of ideas than with creating formally constructed artifacts. Thus, Ellen Green, the mermaid–a triumphant invention–is given room in the novel in hand, *And No Man's Wit;* comments on various minor matters are permitted in *Keeping Up Appearances;* and the amusing ape is given long passages in *The Towers of Trebizond.*

An Assessment

It may be hazarded that her presentation of life, primarily at the level of thought (while not denying its sensuous delights); her complex of tragic awareness and ironic amusement; her constant recognition of the open-endedness of discussions of value; and her care to use language with regard to the authority of its tradition will give much of her work a long contemporaneity.

Notes and References

Chapter One

1. Noel Annan, "The Intellectual Aristocracy," *Studies in Social History*, ed. John Harold Plumb (London, 1955), pp. 254-55, 258.

2. *Letters to a Friend*, edited and with an Introduction by Constance Babington Smith (London, 1961), p. 12 (hereafter cited as *L*. Except where otherwise noted, the information in this biography is drawn from the Introductions to this volume and its sequel [see following note]).

3. *Last Letters to a Friend*, edited and with an Introduction by Constance Babington Smith (London, 1962), p. 616 (hereafter cited as *LL*). Another source of information about her life is *Letters to a Sister*, edited and with an Introduction by Constance Babington Smith (London, 1964), hereafter cited as *S*.

4. Frank Swinnerton, *The Georgian Literary Scene* (London, 1935), p. 298 (hereafter cited as *TGLS*).

5. The details of this relationship are still withheld.

Chapter Two

1. The character of Meyrick is said to be somewhat like that of an interesting black sheep from among the family connections.

2. The "implied author" is discussed by Wayne C. Booth in *The Rhetoric of Fiction* (Chicago, 1961), pp. 70-77: "Just as one's personal letters imply different versions of oneself, depending on the differing relationships with each correspondent and the purpose of each letter, so the writer sets himself out with a different air depending on the needs of particular works" (71).

3. Geoffrey Uther Ellis, *Twilight on Parnassus* (London, 1939), pp. 354-55.

4. In *Views and Vagabonds*, p. 207, Cecil says that Louie has "seen quite wonderfully much already." Whereupon Audrey comments: "I see. You're tackling the problem à la Henry James. His people always sit up so late at night elucidating each other, don't they?" Rizzo (see Bibliography) quotes a letter received by him from Rose Macaulay, dated 1958, in which she said: "It rather interests me someone should have suggested a Jamesian influence in *The Furnace*, as I remember that I was reading him with fascination at the time I wrote it" (9).

5. Kuehn (see Bibliography) calls attention to the historicity of this eruption (31).

6. The Crevequers' superior development of the heart appears to be the reason for their family name: "crève-coeur."

7. See ch. V, sec. 6. In *Views and Vagabonds* (1912), p. 113, Cecil, an enlightened character, speaks enthusiastically of him.

8. The last third of the little book, after the disastrous marriage, consists of realistic dialogue and of allegory; it is much less effective.

9. Northrop Frye, *Anatomy of Criticism* (Princeton, 1957), pp. 308-12. Note especially:

The Menippean satire deals less with people as such than with mental attitudes. . . . The novelist sees evil and folly as social diseases, but the satirist sees them as diseases of the intellect . . . . As the name of an attitude, satire is . . . a combination of fantasy and morality. . . . The short form of the Menippean satire is usually a dialogue or colloquy. . . . Sometimes this form expands to full length . . . : the setting then is usually a *cena* or symposium ["supper" or "dinner"] . . . . A modern development produces the country-house weekends . . . . The word "anatomy" in Burton's title means a dissection or analysis. . . ."

Frye suggests the use of this term for the Menippean satire.

10. Discussed by the present writer in "The Ironic Aesthete and the Sponsoring of Causes: a Rhetorical Quandary in Novelistic Technique," *English Literature in Transition*, X (1966), 39-43.

11. A clipping from what appears to be the publisher's announcement states that Rose Macaulay had written about one-third of this novel before *Views and Vagabonds* (bearing out the present writer's theory that *Views* is a "later" novel). *The Lee Shore* was judged "easily first among the competition novels."

12. See Robert H. Ross, *The Georgian Revolt* (Carbondale, 1965), p. 240.

13. *Coming to London*, ed. John Lehmann (London, 1957), pp. 155-66.

14. Sally and Daphne both engage (offstage) in mild acts of militancy. Mrs. Oliver belongs to a more restrained suffragist organization. Margarete Kluge in "Die Stellung Rose Macaulays zur Frau," *Anglia*, III (June, 1928), 140, pointed out that the only type of woman missing from Rose Macaulay's gallery was the extreme suffragette. Neither are there, however, any criminals.

Chapter Three

1. See *The Westminster Problems Book* (from *Saturday Westmin-*

ster Gazette Competitions, 1904-7), London, 1908; and *The Second Problems Book* (Prizes and Proximes from the *Westminster Gazette,* 1908-9), ed. N. G. Royde Smith, London, 1909.

2. Curiously, in *L,* 48, she says, "The Pond records a summer afternoon in 1919"; the same pond scene appears in *Non-Combatants and Others,* 13-14, in 1916.

Chapter Four

1. Stuart Sherman, *Critical Woodcuts* (New York, 1926), p. 83.

2. Elizabeth Bowen, in her section of *Coming to London* (see ch. II, n. 13), p. 79; Mary Ellen Chase, "Five Literary Portraits," *Massachusetts Review,* III (Spring, 1962), 515-16.

3. Reviewed by Katherine Mansfield, *Athenaeum,* April 11, 1919, pp. 173-74.

4. Margot Brussow, *Zeitbedingtes in den Werken Rose Macaulays,* a published dissertation (Griefswald, 1934), p. 8. Karin Michaëlis, *Den farlige Alder* (Copenhagen, 1910); published in English in 1912.

5. Cyril Connolly, *The Condemned Playground, Essays: 1927-1944* (New York, 1946), p. 117. See also *Times Literary Supplement,* November 27, 1924, p. 794, and Joseph Wood Krutch, *Saturday Review of Literature,* I (February 28, 1925), 555.

6. This political skepticism is discussed in Irmgard Wahl's *Gesellschaftskritik und Skeptizismus bei Rose Macaulay,* a published dissertation (Tübingen, 1936), pp. 73-79.

7. See also "Does Ancestry Matter?" (in the series "Who I Am"), *Daily Express,* June 5, 1928.

8. Herbert George Wells, "Popular Writers and Press Critics," *Saturday Review,* LXXXI (February 8, 1896), 145.

9. Gilbert Thomas, *Spectator,* CXLV (October 4, 1930), 741; see also Raymond Mortimer, *Nation and Athenaeum,* XLVII (September 27, 1930), 796.

Chapter Five

1. See also "Losing One's Books," *Spectator,* CLXVII (November 7, 1941), 444-45, reprinted as "Book-Building after a Blitz," in *Saturday Review of Literature,* XXV (June 6, 1942), 15-16.

2. Reviewed by Bonamy Dobrée, *Spectator,* CXLVII (September 19, 1931), 360; *Times Literary Supplement,* August 6, 1931, p. 607; Edith C. Batho, *Review of English Studies,* IX (July, 1933), 357.

3. Cicely Veronica Wedgwood, Introduction to *They Were Defeated* (London, 1960).

4. See also *New Statesman and Nation*, IV (October 22, 1932), 492-93; Humbert Wolfe, *Observer*, October 16, 1932, p. 5; Christopher Morley, *Saturday Review of Literature*, IX (October 29, 1932), 205; Richard Church, *Growth of the English Novel* (London, 1951), p. 145.

5. See Anthony Burgess, "The Pattern and the Core," *Spectator*, CCXV (July 2, 1965), 20; in this article, written thirty-one years later, he observed: "Her *Minor Pleasures* is remembered while, I fear, even the author of the companion volume on Major Pleasures is forgotten."

6. Harold Nicolson and others, "The Pleasures of Knowing Rose Macaulay," *Encounter*, XII (March, 1959), 23-31.

7. See William Plomer, *Spectator*, CLIII (July 6, 1934) 26; Edith H. Walton, "Rose Macaulay's Kindly Satire," *New York Times Book Review*, August 19, 1934, p. 6. The present writer discussed this novel in "The Skeptical Balance: a Study of Rose Macaulay's *Going Abroad*," *Papers of the Michigan Academy of Science, Arts, and Letters*, XLVIII (1963), 675-88.

8. See also her review of Lionel Trilling's *E. M. Forster* in *Horizon*, X (December, 1944), 432-34.

9. *The English Novelists*, ed. Derek Verschoyle (London, 1936).

10. See also "Mr. Joad and the P. P. U.," *New Statesman and Nation*, XIII (May 22, 1937), 844-45.

11. Kate O'Brien, in her review in *Spectator*, CLXIV (June 21, 1940), 844, thought Ellen "surely should have had a whole novel to herself. . . . It seems very wasteful of a rich and lovely idea."

Chapter Six

1. As often, in teasing clergymen, she quotes from hymns or from the liturgy.

2. Rose Macaulay had wished to entitle her book *Ora Maritima* ("seacoast"), after a fourth-century Roman poem based on a Greek topographical book of the sixth century B.C. describing this shore.

3. She evokes the final lines of Matthew Arnold's "The Scholar Gypsy."

4. These letters revealed her clandestine love-relationship. Among her remarks on this novel is: "I think you are right about my Wilderness being largely an unconscious prayer" (*L*, 292).

5. Seven years after her death a greatly abridged version of this work was issued, edited by Constance Babington Smith and interpreted in photographs by Roloff Beny (London: Thames and Hudson, 1965).

6. According to her editor, Mark Bonham Carter (see ch. V, n. 6).

7. Rose Macaulay had used the first person in only one other novel, *Potterism*, and then only in parts.

8. *Anatomy of Criticism* (see ch. II, n. 9), p. 308.

9. This includes a private joke: Rose Macaulay's own Morris was stolen under the same circumstances on January 19, 1955; and for the next two wintry months (during her seventy-fourth year), she rode her wartime bicycle through mid-London traffic.

Chapter Seven

1. Frank Swinnerton, *Spectator*, CLXXXIV (May 12, 1950), 653.

2. Rose Macaulay, *Times Literary Supplement*, April 6, 1951, p. 208.

3. Reginald Brimley Johnson, *Some Contemporary Novelists— Women* (London, 1920), p. 65.

Selected Bibliography

PRIMARY SOURCES

All references in the text are to the first English editions. The first American publishers are noted in parentheses; any differences in title or date are indicated.

1. Novels:

Abbots Verney. London: John Murray, 1906.

The Furnace. London: John Murray, 1907.

The Secret River. London: John Murray, 1909.

The Valley Captives. London: John Murray, 1911.

Views and Vagabonds. London: John Murray, 1912.

The Lee Shore. London: Hodder and Stoughton, 1912.

The Making of a Bigot. London: Hodder and Stoughton, 1914.

Non-Combatants and Others. London: Hodder and Stoughton, 1916.

What Not: a Prophetic Comedy. London: Constable, 1918.

Potterism: a Tragi-Farcical Tract. London: William Collins, 1920. (New York: Boni and Liveright.)

Dangerous Ages. London: William Collins, 1921. (New York: Boni and Liveright.)

Mystery at Geneva. London: William Collins, 1922. (New York: Boni and Liveright, 1923.)

Told by an Idiot. London: William Collins, 1923. (New York: Boni and Liveright, 1924.)

Orphan Island. London: William Collins, 1924. (New York: Boni and Liveright, 1925.)

Crewe Train. London: William Collins, 1926. (New York: Boni and Liveright.)

Keeping Up Appearances. London: William Collins, 1928. (*Daisy and Daphne.* New York: Boni and Liveright.)

Staying with Relations. London: William Collins, 1930. (New York: Horace Liveright.)

They Were Defeated. London: William Collins, 1932. (*The Shadow Flies.* New York: Harper and Brothers.)

Going Abroad. London: William Collins, 1934. (New York: Harper and Brothers.)

I Would Be Private. London: William Collins, 1937. (New York: Harper and Brothers.)

And No Man's Wit. London: William Collins, 1940. (Boston: Little, Brown and Company.)

The World My Wilderness. London: William Collins, 1950. (Boston: Little, Brown and Company.)

The Towers of Trebizond. London: William Collins, 1956. (New York: Farrar, Straus and Cudahy, 1957.)

2. Poetry:

The Two Blind Countries. London: Sidgwick and Jackson, 1914.

Three Days. London: Constable, 1919.

3. Essays, Criticism:

A Casual Commentary. London: Methuen, 1925. (New York: Boni and Liveright, 1926.)

Catchwords and Claptrap. London: Hogarth Press, 1926.

Some Religious Elements in English Literature. London: Hogarth Press, 1931. (New York: Harcourt, Brace.)

Milton. London: Duckworth, 1934. (New York: Harper and Brothers, 1935.)

Personal Pleasures. London: Victor Gollancz, 1935. (New York: Macmillan Company, 1936.)

The Writings of E. M. Forster. London: Hogarth Press, 1938. (New York: Harcourt, Brace.)

4. History, Travel:

Life among the English. London: William Collins, 1942.

They Went to Portugal. London: Jonathan Cape, 1946.

Fabled Shore: from the Pyrenees to Portugal. London: Hamish Hamilton, 1949. (New York: Farrar, Straus.)

Pleasure of Ruins. London: Weidenfeld and Nicolson, 1953. (New York: Walker, 1966.)

5. Anthology:

The Minor Pleasures of Life. London: Victor Gollancz, 1934. (New York: Harper and Brothers, 1935.)

6. Letters:

Letters to a Friend: 1950-1952, ed. CONSTANCE BABINGTON SMITH. London: William Collins, 1961. (New York: Atheneum, 1962.)

Last Letters to a Friend: 1952-1958, ed. CONSTANCE BABINGTON SMITH. London: William Collins, 1962. (New York: Atheneum, 1963.)

Letters to a Sister from Rose Macaulay, ed. CONSTANCE BABINGTON SMITH. London: Collins, 1964. (New York: Atheneum.)

7. Articles (Autobiographical):

"Auto-Obituary," (see ch. IV, sec. 1); "Coming to London," (see ch. II, sec. 8); "What I Believe," (see ch. V, sec. 7); "Writing," (see ch. V, sec. 4).

Selected Bibliography

SECONDARY SOURCES

There have been no full-length published studies of Rose Macaulay. Two unpublished American dissertations are listed here; and two published German dissertations, written halfway through Rose Macaulay's career, are listed in the Notes (ch. IV, 4 and 6). Some seventy-eight reviews in periodicals or critiques in books are referred to in the text or Notes, in connection with the work under discussion. The following list points out some especially useful sources.

1. Bibliography:

RIZZO, PHILIP LOUIS. "Rose Macaulay: A Critical Survey." Unpublished dissertation, University of Pennsylvania, 1959. The writer has gathered an extremely useful list of primary and secondary sources. The critical survey emphasizes the satirical novels. The writer lacked, of course, the biographical materials that became available in the 1960's.

2. Criticism and Biography:

INGLISHAM, JOHN. "Rose Macaulay," *Bookman*, LXXII (May, 1927), 107-10. He defends her "humanity," "charm," and "poetry" against those who overstress her satire.

KUEHN, ROBERT EARL. "The Pleasures of Rose Macaulay: An Introduction to Her Novels." Unpublished dissertation, University of Wisconsin, 1962. The bibliography adds a few works to Rizzo's list. The dissertation, to some extent a commentary on Rizzo's, constitutes a perceptive discussion of the novels.

"Miss Macaulay's Novels" (Anon. rev.). *Times Literary Supplement*, May 12, 1950, p. 292. To a review of *The World My Wilderness* the writer adds a thoughtful survey of the novels back to *Potterism* (1920).

NICOLSON, HAROLD, and ROSAMUND LEHMANN, ALAN PRYCE-JONES, DWIGHT MACDONALD, PATRICK KINROSS, C. V. WEDGWOOD, MARK BONHAM CARTER, ANTHONY POWELL, WILLIAM PLOMER, DIANA COOPER. "The Pleasures of Knowing Rose Macaulay," *Encounter*, XII (March, 1959), 23-31. Each friend offers a memorial sketch.

NICOLSON, HAROLD. "Spanish Journey," *Observer*, May 6, 1949, p. 291. This review gives a good assessment of Rose Macaulay as a travel writer.

PRYCE-JONES, ALAN. Introduction to the 1960 edition of *Orphan Island*. London: Collins. This lively account gives a sense of the spirit of the woman and her work.

SMITH, CONSTANCE BABINGTON. Introductions to *Letters to a Friend, Last Letters to a Friend*, and *Letters to a Sister* (see Primary Sources). This biographical information, written by a younger cousin of Rose Macaulay, is based on firsthand knowledge, consultation with other relatives and friends, and study of documents. It is sensitively and accurately presented.

STEWART, DOUGLAS G. *The Ark of God: Studies in Five Modern Novelists, James Joyce, Aldous Huxley, Graham Greene, Rose Macaulay, Joyce Cary.* London: Carey Kingsgate Press, 1961. He discusses her "Anglicanism" and "deep earnestness."

SWINNERTON, FRANK. "Rose Macaulay," *Kenyon Review,* XXIX (November, 1967), 591-608. The writer repeats details from his earlier passages and considers her work in relation to her social class.

————. *The Georgian Literary Scene.* London: William Heinemann, 1935. This friend of the author devotes several pages to sketching her as a woman and as a writer.

Index

DATE DUE

GAYLORD			PRINTED IN U.S.A.